Home on the Range:

Growing up on Teesside in the 50s and 60s

About the Author

Susan Lewis CBE was born in 1947 in Stokesley Crescent, Billingham, the daughter of Ken and Elsie Lewis. She attended Billingham South Infants and Junior School, followed by Henry Smith School in Hartlepool. After studying at the University of Newcastle upon Tyne and the University of Sheffield, Susan taught at various secondary schools in Yorkshire where she held a number of senior management positions. She moved to Wales in 1986 to broaden her career by becoming a school inspector and in 1997 she become the first woman to be appointed HM Chief Inspector of Education and Training in Wales. Susan was awarded the CBE in 2008 for services to education.

Home on the Range:
Growing up on Teesside in the 50s and 60s

by Susan Lewis

www.6epublishing.net

First published in paperback in 2011
by Sixth Element Publishing
Arthur Robinson House
13-14 The Green
Billingham TS23 1EU
Tel: 01642 360253

ISBN 978-1-908299-00-0

British Library Cataloguing in Publication Data. A catalogue record for this book is available from the British Library.

Printed in Great Britain.

www.6epublishing.net

Contents

Introduction

Early stories and memories 1

Billeted in Wales 12

The street 16

Life at home 20

Gardens and gardening 28

The shed 30

Food, drink and shopping.............................33

Eating out...46

Radio, music, books and television.............49

The cinema..57

The club...60

School 63

Sayings, superstitions and etiquette............90

Health..95

Church and religion 99

Events and celebrations 104

Sights, sounds and smells........................... 107

Holiday times... 113

Brands, adverts and jingles 119

Fashion.. 122

Work and money 124

A few final words 130

Introduction

I started to write this book in 1991 just after my father had died. It was that awful period when, well into my adulthood, I realised that I was an orphan. I could no longer rely on my father's eight and a half decade memory. My story now had to be what I could recall unsupported by parental tales.

My first attempt at writing was short lived and I only tried again when I retired in 2008. This is the final result of my efforts. The story does not pretend to be an objective history of the 50s and 60s, many others far better qualified have written that. It is a personal account of what I recall and feel about those times at home in Billingham and at school in Hartlepool. It is written from a distance in miles and time. The story is presented thematically and with great affection for people and places that have shaped my life. I am surprised at how much I have remembered. At the same time, I am slightly disconcerted at the influence that the people, places and events have had on my life.

I hope that you find the book strikes a chord with you as you journey with me from post-war austerity to 1960s optimism, liberation and prosperity: what history may decide was a golden age in the last century.

My thanks go to good friends who have encouraged me in this project and helped with checking the manuscript and supplying a few of the photographs.

Early stories and memories

I was born in 1947, nine months on from what is always referred to when people are talking about the depth of snowdrifts, the persistence of ice and freezing temperatures: the worst winter in living memory. I grew up thinking everything happened either before or after 'The War'. My parents seemed to me to be old. Mam was 43 when she gave birth to me, her second child. My father was 42. Both had been married before, neither marriage lasting long but for different reasons.

Mam (Elsie) was born in Hull. She was the seventh of eight children and the youngest girl. She married her first husband Clarence Stonehouse, a warehouseman in a lemonade factory, on 30 January 1932. The following year, on 28 September 1933, she was called to the place where Clarence worked to identify his body which lay casually covered with a sheet in the corridor of the factory. Clarence had died at work from a lung haemorrhage caused by tuberculosis.

Mam in the 1930s.

Dad (Ken) was born in Llandebie, Carmarthenshire, South Wales, the son of a policeman. He was the youngest son and the third of seven children, two of whom died in infancy. Against the advice of his sisters, he married his first wife on 4 December 1927. Shortly after, his wife ran off with the manager of one of the cinemas in Llanelli and he never saw her again. Following this, Dad left Wales and went to live and work all over England and Scotland. He only returned to Wales at 80 years of age coming to live with me when I

Dad walking on the North Yorkshire Moors. Photograph taken about 1940 by Dick Ramage, my brother Tony's godfather. Dick was pharmacy manager at Boots the Chemists in Stockton and a friend of Dad's.

moved to the Swansea area for work.

Mam and Dad met at a dance in the Winter Gardens, Blackpool when they were each on holiday in the mid-1930s. They corresponded with each other over a period of time and afterwards set up home together, eventually settling in Norton in Teesside in 1939 when Dad got a job as an electric welder in ICI. He was known in ICI and by all his mates as Taff.

It was not long before my older brother Tony was born in August 1941. His arrival was followed by an event which was to determine where my family lived for many years to come.

Within hours of Tony being born at 6 Malden Road, Norton, a German bomber dropped what I understand was a parachute mine in between rows of houses in nearby Benson and Pine Streets. The exploding mine

destroyed houses in a hundred metre stretch around those streets and damaged houses in Malden Road. It also blew out windows up to a mile away and caused many casualties. Dad was out at the time of the blast carrying out air raid warden duties. He returned home

One of the earliest pictures of Tony taken in 1943 when he was about 18 months old.

Tony aged about 2 or 3. The picture was taken around 1944 in Thirlwell Ltd, a photographic studio in Stockton-on-Tees.

to find his own house badly damaged. In fact, there was serious damage to every room in the place apart from the room where Mam and Tony were.

The newly-born Tony was wrapped up in a blanket in a Moses basket that Mam had thankfully pushed under the bed when the explosions started. The midwife, who had delivered Tony at home only hours before, burst into tears when she saw the dust-covered baby in the basket. She thought that he had been killed by the blast. But Tony cleaned up well and lived to tell the tale of his early escapade.

About 20 people were made homeless in that overnight bombing. The Lewises were amongst them and they had to move. Within a few weeks, Mam and Dad found a house for rent about a mile away in Billingham on a large estate built and owned then by Imperial Chemical Industries (ICI). Our lives in Stokesley Crescent had begun. The weekly rent payable to ICI for the house in 1941 was nine shillings and seven pence (just under 50p), ten old pence (less than 5p) of which was for water rates. Some 40 years later, when ICI sold their housing stock to The Bradford Property Trust (irreverently referred to by Dad as the Property Twist) the rent was £10.30.

I was part of the post war baby boom, born at home in one of our front bedrooms with a local midwife in attendance. For years after, the midwife would stop and speak to Mam and me in the street as she did her rounds on her regulation black bike. A basket attached to the handlebars of her bike contained a black leather bag with all the tools of her trade. She cut a formal figure in her uniform of dark blue gabardine coat and brimmed round hat, but she was always friendly and wanted to know how everyone was doing.

The rosewood Edwardian double bed in which I and my brother were born was part of a magnificent bedroom suite that belonged to my mother's eldest sister, Gertrude (Auntie Gertie). The suite, which I

This photo is the earliest one I have of me, taken around 1949-1950. It is one of a number of tiny Polyphotos taken in studios probably somewhere in Stockton. I do not recall the toy so perhaps it was one provided in the photographer's studio to amuse small children in front of the camera.

still have, was a wedding gift and leaving present from Hammonds the furniture store in Hull at a time when women had to stop working when they married.

Auntie Gertie lived with us for a few years after she was widowed. I do not have a clear picture of her. Dad said she was rather gloomy and inclined to complain, but then perhaps she was grieving for her husband who had died not long since, and maybe she was just unwell as she herself died of cachexia and stomach cancer aged 56 in April 1950. The main memory I have of Auntie Gertie is of her teaching me to read whilst I was a toddler. I remember reading 'The Little Red Hen' with her, delighting in the repetition of, 'Not I', said the goose, cat, and the dog.

Beyond the memories of Auntie Gertie's reading legacy, my earliest memories have to be the ones in which my mother features as she died when I was seven and my brother was 13. Sadly, these memories are few in number and inconsequential enough to make me wonder why I recall them at all and in such precise detail. They appear in my mind like those sepia, dreamlike, slowed-down shots you see in films when the intention is to take you back to happier times.

I have no real image of Mam as a person, just of events and things that happened when she was there. These memories include silly little incidents like sitting on the draining board whilst Mam rubbed butter on my skin to remove the tar stains I had acquired from sitting popping tar bubbles on the newly-surfaced road on a hot day.

Mam made all our clothes using an old black Singer sewing machine. The machine was set into a table and operated by foot using a treadle. I can recall her peering through glasses to see the needle well enough to thread it. She did smocking on the front of my dresses and made Tony's shirts out of the backs of Dad's shirts that had worn out.

I remember being with Mam while she was talking to other adults, either at the shops or at home. She would chat to the neighbours and I would only half understand things that were said. I recall shuffling about holding my Mam's hand and feeling rather bored as she talked to someone she had met in Station Road on the way to the shops in Billingham Village. However, why I have a particularly clear memory of a day when she stopped to talk to someone by the underground toilets in the Memorial Gardens in Station Road, and why I found the thick opaque glass squares that formed the roof of the toilets so fascinating, I have no idea.

There were happy times with Mam and Dad in our back garden in Billingham. We would gingerly pick blackberries (or brambles as we called them) from the bushes that grew along the fence between our house and number 49 where my godparents Mr and Mrs Walker lived with their grown up children Ken and Margaret.

I am not sure whether I was more afraid of the thorns or the wasps and bees that were all over the bushes.

I also recall playing in the back garden on the swing that my father had made for me. I say made, but it was more like partly made. The frame was a substantial tubular metal affair that was welded to last forever – welding being my Dad's trade. In the absence of wood for a seat, Dad suspended a length of washing line from the two sides of the top and slung over it a flock-filled cushion to make a seat. Dad could make anything in metal to last a lifetime, but if it required any wooden parts as finishing or refinement, you could forget it. For years, we had a fine stainless steel coal shovel that was never finished off with its wooden handle. The shovel was freezing cold to hold on winter days when you had to go out to fill the coal scuttle from the coal house.

I took this photograph of Dad in his work clothes (trousers tucked into his socks) in the back garden in Stokesley Crescent in the late 1950s. The camera was a rudimentary affair, little more than a pinhole camera in a plastic box. The pictures were the same size as the negatives. If you look closely you can see the prefabs in Lunedale Road in the background.

Tony aged about 9 or 10 and like most boys of this age he is just growing into his teeth.

Me aged about 3 or 4.

There was a metal clothes prop too. Everyone else had a wooden clothes prop, but we had a long, heavy metal affair that was so weighty it would have knocked you out, or worse, if it had fallen on you.

I had a much-loved tricycle that Tony tried to borrow for a ride himself and I had decided he should not be on the trike. As he teased me, I hit him in frustration, striking him awkwardly so that his teeth cut through his lip making him bleed profusely. I was very upset and frightened by the blood. So was he. I hated it when he was hurt, as he often seemed to be because he suffered badly from nosebleeds. I can remember him stretched out on the floor in the front room, blood pouring from his nose while Mam placed a cold back door key at the back of his neck. Quite how this medical procedure was meant to work, I am not sure. Thinking back, he would have been more likely to choke than anything else.

A guilty early memory is the time when, aged about 7, I discovered a beautiful doll in the wardrobe in Mam and Dad's room just before Christmas. The doll was dressed in a lovely knitted blue-hooded coat over a handmade white dress, and knitted pants and vest. My brother told me I had to leave the doll where it was and say nothing to anyone. Lo and behold, on Christmas morning, the doll turned up in the pillowcase we put at the end of my bed and no one except Tony and I ever knew I had already seen the doll.

Tony and I had not known that although Mam and Dad had lived together as man and wife for about 20 years, they had not married until the 1950s. Whilst Mam had been a widow and free to marry, Dad had been tied to his first marriage partly because of the expense involved in a divorce and also because he did not know where his first wife was. To employ someone to search for her would have meant more expense. By the late 1940s, Dad heard from someone in Wales that his first wife had died. However, this proved to be incorrect as he received a letter from her via a solicitor requesting a divorce as she wished to remarry. Even though Dad's wife had left him, the divorce with its solicitor's fees was expensive. The sum involved amounted to about 20 times more than Dad's weekly earnings. He borrowed money from his employer to pay for the divorce and had to pay back the loan week-by-week over a period of years.

The divorce came through in December 1954 and in January 1955, Mam and Dad married at Stockton Register Office aged 50 and 49 respectively. What might under other circumstances have been a happy affair was presumably a bitter-sweet experience as Mam had just discovered in 1954 that she had cervical cancer. She found this out in a very cruel and unusual way. Dad was in the throes of doing the washing up when a letter arrived from a hospital in Newcastle. Dad picked it up and

This is my last school photo at Billingham Infants' School taken in early summer 1955. I was treated to a home perm for this occasion. The dress was the last one made by Mam. It was pale turquoise with white flowers with black centres and darker blue-green stems.

put the letter by the sink while he finished what he was doing. He had recently attended a hospital in Newcastle for dental treatment and, seeing the postmark, assumed the letter was for him.

Unfortunately, before Dad had chance to open the letter, Mam came in, saw the letter and realised it was addressed to her. She opened it and read what was a letter intended for her GP and sent in error to Mam at our address. It was clear from the letter that she was terminally ill and that she had not long to live. Treatment for cervical cancer in those days was virtually non-existent and it was one of the biggest causes of death of women in the UK.

Mam lived as a married woman for just over six months. After a painful last few weeks, she died at home in July 1955 aged 51.

Following the discovery of the cancer, life changed dramatically for all of us. Dad, who had started work on the day of his 14th birthday, thought that Tony (soon to be 14) was grown up and so he stayed with Mam and Dad alone at home. Palliative care was rudimentary in the 1950s. Being with Mam in her last days as she struggled with the immense pain of her cancer was something that haunted both Dad and Tony all their lives. Tony said he used to lie upstairs in bed jamming the pillows around his head to try to drown out the sounds of Mam screaming in agony.

As a seven year old, I was oblivious of how ill Mam was. A couple of weeks before she died, I was sent away to stay with one of her brothers – Walter and his wife Nora – in Hull. Uncle Walter came to our house and took me by train to his small terraced house in Hull. I had never met either him or his wife before and had never been away from home without both parents and my brother. The days passed with me helping Auntie Nora with the housework and shopping. One day, Uncle Walter took me out for a walk around Hull. This tour of the town culminated in our visiting the police station and being shown around the cells. In retrospect, it seems odd to take a small child, who was in a strange place because of dire circumstances at home, for a day out to the local police station. I thought he must have worked there, but he was actually a railwayman.

One Sunday morning, Auntie Nora came to tell me that they had had a telegram to say that my mother had gone to live with Jesus. Despite my time at Sunday school I did not fully understand what this meant, but it did not sound good.

Some days later, I went to stay with an old friend of Mam's in another part of Hull. I was spoiled and slept in a large bed with a silk cover on it. Then, to my delight, Dad turned up, but he was sad and not his usual cheerful self. Together we went from Hull, not home, but on a train to stay in Llanelli with Dad's sister Isabel and her husband.

I had never been to Llanelli before, but I liked Dad's sister Isabel and her husband Eric. They were uncomplicated, generous and full of fun. They had come up to Billingham a few years earlier to stay with us and delighted in eating Mam's homemade bread and pastries as fast as she could make them. Eric, who had come up to the North East for Mam's funeral, had taken Tony down to Llanelli on the exhausting 13+ hour train journey that it was in those days. Dad, Tony and I spent a couple of weeks in Llanelli, going to the beach, the local markets, and visiting Dad's other sisters Vera and Violet (Vi) in Carmarthen before we returned home on the train to Billingham.

Back in Billingham, life was very strange without Mam. The house seemed empty, bleak and strangely quiet. Things that had been in the house the last time I was there, like the piano Mam had played, had gone.

I could not really believe that Mam was dead. In any case, I am not sure that I understood what dead meant. Nobody spoke about her yet I used to imagine that I saw her in a crowd in Stockton. I would look closely and then realise it was not her after all. At other times, I thought that the door would just open and in she would walk.

Auntie Vi.

Dad found it hard to go to work and do all the things like shopping, cooking and cleaning. Tony and I did jobs to help, but in the early autumn, Auntie Vi, Dad's unmarried sister, came up from South Wales to Billingham to be our housekeeper.

Vi was not a bit like Mam. She put wallpaper on the wrong way up and bought unsuitable curtains. She was unpredictable, fiery and short-tempered, but at the same time full of fun and very generous with her money. She bought me a pair of roller skates when it was not my birthday or Christmas. At other times she would give you half a crown at the drop of a hat, or ply you with sweets and ice cream on visits to the cinema.

Auntie Vi smoked, a thing unknown in our house until her arrival. She liked Canadian cigarettes called Du Maurier which came in a flat red box with an art deco design on the lid. Perhaps she had acquired this seemingly sophisticated habit whilst working for the Navy, Army and Air Force Institute (NAAFI) in West Wales where American and Canadian airmen were stationed.

Not long after she arrived with us, Vi started to see someone she had known from years before – Jackie Layton, a James Cagney lookalike. Jackie Layton had been based down in West Wales during his spell in the army.

In the following spring of 1956, aged 45, Violet Margaret Brittania Lewis married Hubert Jackie Layton.

I liked Jackie Layton well enough. When he visited, he did tricks that amused a 9 year old. He could make sixpences disappear and reappear and cause a small wooden bird to blow smoke rings from a lighted rolled up piece of paper in its beak.

Dad and Jackie Layton did not get on. Dad thought Jackie was a waster and so once they were married, Auntie Vi and husband moved to Norton to live with Jackie's stepmother, a kindly soul called Mrs Flowers. Jackie, it seemed, had borrowed money from Dad and my brother had the wretched task of going each week to the rough Blue Hall estate in Norton to collect the debt.

In the November of 1956, Vi gave

Tony aged about 16 (early 1958)
holding our youngest cousin,
Jack (Kenneth Anthony) Layton
outside Jack's father's house in
Somerset Road.

birth to a baby boy, Jack Kenneth Anthony, named after all the closest men in her life.

Our cousin was sadly only about 4 months old when his mother died. Young Jackie was left to be brought up mainly by his step grandmother.

Stokesley Crescent was getting to be a dangerous place to live. Two significant figures in our lives had gone in less than two years.

On the day of Auntie Vi's funeral, I was out playing in the street. I can even remember what I was wearing: a camel coloured duffel coat and a pair of tartan trousers (so-called trews). At the point when people were all about to go to the funeral, I think that they realised that they could not leave me without anyone at home or in my godparents' house. So, dressed as I was, I was bundled into the funeral car and before I knew it was sitting squashed up in a pew in St Cuthbert's Church.

Billeted in Wales

By March 1957, when Vi died, Dad was finding it hard to cope with a 9 year old and so I was dispatched to live in Llanelli with Auntie Isabel and her husband Eric and my cousins.

Uncle Denton, Dad's brother from South Wales, who had come for Vi's funeral, took me to Wales on the train. Denton was a second generation policeman. Unlike Dad, he was dour and rather disconcerting. He hardly spoke at all on our long journey to Llanelli. I was transfixed by his enormous black shiny boots and his long arms and huge hands, which seemed too large for his jacket. I stayed in Llanelli for about six months from March to late August 1957.

Cousins David (Winston), Heather and Terry.

All my memories there are of lazy warm days and of the love and care of Auntie Isabel and Uncle Eric.

I learned how to grow and pick tomatoes, cucumbers and kidney beans in the minute greenhouse and cold frame that effectively formed the rear

Uncle Eric and Auntie Isabel.

garden. I played with the dogs and cat, taking the younger terrier for walks. We had visits to the beach to sunbathe, fish and pick cockles. The terrier would embarrass us by fetching the clothes of people who had gone for a swim. We walked past the docks to get to the beach and saw the many grey battleships moored there after the Suez Crisis. We went to Carmarthen to see my Dad's other sister Auntie Vera and her family, usually on market day when we could buy fresh produce from the many stalls.

Most nights, I would go with Isabel, and sometimes Eric, to a local whist drive, as popular in the 1950s as bingo was to become later. The night of the week denoted where the whist drive was held. One night was the Fire Station. Other nights it was the Thomas Arms. At the Thomas Arms, a chirpy chain-smoking Cockney called Charlie ran the whist drive. There were regulars at these whist drives and the tension in some of the games was palpable, with fallings out over poor leading of suits and so on in the rounds of whist. After I grew bored with watching the adults play cards, I would drift off to play with other children whose parents or relatives had brought them along. If I was lucky, I sold raffle tickets around the tables and was allowed to keep the small change if the punters were feeling generous.

I was fascinated to watch Uncle Eric shave with a cut throat razor at a mirror over the kitchen sink. My cousins would joke as if to bump into him, but never did. I also marvelled at how thinly Eric could cut a joint of meat at Sunday lunchtime, transferring his stropping and sharpening skills from the razor to the carving knife in preparation. Auntie Isabel could do something similar with bread, clutching the already buttered loaf to her pinafore just under her bosom and producing very thin and even slices.

Whilst I was living with Auntie Isabel and Uncle Eric, I went to the school that my Dad and Isabel had attended for a while during their own childhood. Lakefield School was in the same street in which Isabel and family lived. Eric was the school caretaker and Isabel the cleaner at the school. Mr Williams, a ruddy-faced Welsh-speaking smallholder from the nearby village of Trimsaren was my class teacher. In another guise, he arrived at Isabel's house once a week in the evening on his bike selling a glut of vegetables from his smallholding. In class, he was kindly enough and tried to settle me in, but I did not like being at school there.

The school was very old and the teachers seemed very fierce. I did not like the look of the canes that rested readily on the teachers' high desks. My legs had bruises, not from the canes but from bashing them on the metal frames of the old-fashioned trestle desks. I recall having a test in Welsh and getting one out of ten. The word I got right was 'ci' – dog in Welsh. I got this correct not because of what I had learnt at school, but because I had heard Uncle Eric cursing the dog when it got in his way at home. Mr Williams, in his rather flatfooted, but seemingly supportive, way, used my score to demonstrate to the several others in his class who had none out of ten that even Susan, from the North of England, had managed to get one right.

As a scrawny child with a strange accent, I must have been a bit of an oddity. However, I had some street 'cred' because I could stay in school after everyone else had gone to help my Aunt and Uncle to clean the school. That bit, I did like. I was intrigued by the foreign, smoke-smelling world of the staff room when the teachers had left. Best of all, I relished being able to borrow books over the weekend from the library and Uncle Eric would return them on Monday morning before anyone knew they had gone. I was particularly delighted one Friday evening to bring home a pristine copy of the story of Pinocchio newly arrived in a large wooden crate from the school library service. I can remember reading the book in bed with the sash window pushed halfway down allowing in the street sounds on an idyllic warm summer evening.

Out in the schoolyard, we were forbidden to play on the fire escape, but we did. One day as the whistle blew for the end of afternoon break, I jumped down from three steps up only to fall and hit my knee on the last step. The pain was great, the cut was deep and the blood ran down my leg and onto my white ankle socks. Nevertheless, I did not dare react in case there was an inquiry into how the accident had happened. I was doing alright until the eagle-eyed teacher on duty spotted my blood red sock as I limped from the yard. My offence was discovered, but my connection to the school caretaker paid off yet again and nothing was said before I was cleaned up and sent back to class. Later that afternoon, however, on my way home with Auntie Isabel, I tripped up and fell over as we walked along the uneven pavement. Oh, how it hurt to fall on the recent injury! I howled twice as much to make up for not having made a murmur in the yard.

During the summer holiday, I joined my cousin and his parents in cleaning the school ready for the teachers and pupils to return in September. We sang hymns or pop songs of the time, like 'Unchained Melody', loudly and in harmony as we systematically cleaned each room. We dusted everything and then swept the floors after sprinkling them with a damp sandy substance that trapped the dust. Once cleaned, the rooms were locked up for the rest of the holidays. The messiest job was whitewashing the outside toilets. This was men's work and although I was allowed to stir the whitewash mixture in the galvanised bucket, it was down to Uncle Eric or my cousin to venture into the strange world of the urinals to paint the walls. They came home later, covered in tiny white splashes over their faces and tanned arms.

I must have been at school in Llanelli for only about four months during the summer term of 1957. It seemed like years. During the summer holidays to my great relief, Dad decided that I should come home, as I would soon be in the year leading to the 11 plus. How pleased I was to be going home even though I knew I would miss Auntie Isabel and family.

The street

Around the late 1920s and through the 1930s, ICI, the biggest employer in Billingham, built several large estates to house its workers and managers. Our workers' estate, built around 1928, was regarded as one of the better ones as it was furthest away from and upwind from the smellier parts of ICI's chemical production. The estate lay to the north side of the main estate road, Central Avenue. On a map, our part of the estate has the outline of an alien's head, like something out of Dan Dare. Apart from my brief sojourn in Wales, I lived for my first 17 years in Stokesley Crescent, Billingham, in the house in which I was born.

The houses were built in short terraces of up to ten properties. Ours was one of two in the centre of a run of ten set back off the road. In front of the houses, between the main pavement and road, was a fenced-off grassed area about the size of a tennis court. The grassed area was known as 'the square'. There were a number of squares around the estate. In fact, one day coming home from school, I absentmindedly

Dad on right outside 51 Stokesley Crescent and godmother, Mrs Walker, outside number 49. Picture taken in the 1980s.

went to the wrong house in a symmetrically similar part of the estate, mistaking it for ours.

Children were not supposed to play in the square, but we did. Why else would you put a large grassed area in front of our houses? We climbed over the fence into the square or else squeezed through a gap or broken part in the fence. Tales were told of nasty neighbours who lived around other squares and confiscated balls and prevented children from playing there. This did not happen much in Stokesley Crescent. The mothers around the square saw to that. Even in the relatively car free days of the 1950s they felt that children were safer playing in the square than in the road. Sometimes in the summer holidays, the mothers organised a sports day and we used the pathway around the square as a natural running track. We were treated to biscuits and orange juice made from watered down concentrate supplied by the National Health Service to post war babies.

We also played in the road, especially if the grass in the square had not been cut for a while. Very few neighbours had cars and we hardly ever had to stop play because of cars or commercial vehicles. We would play all kinds of games depending on what was in vogue at any time of the year and whether or not anyone had a ball. It might be hopscotch, which for reasons unknown was called itchy-bay. It might be whip and top, yo-yo or hoola-hoop. Many games were variations of tag or hide and seek.

One favourite game involved having an empty tin can in the middle of the road with three short pieces of firewood balanced across the can top. We children split into two opposing sides and the plan was for members of one side to aim a ball at the can scattering the sticks. Once the can was knocked over, the members of the other side had to set up the can and sticks without being hit with the ball. If the ball hit a player, the player had to sit out. Rounds of the game went on until the whole of one side was out.

We also played marbles or alleys. We used the gutters as runs for the marbles and avoiding the marbles going down the drains was all part of the fun. Skipping with a long length of washing line across the road was popular as was juggling or bouncing and catching two or three balls (two-baller or three-baller) up against the house wall.

Towards the top end of Stokesley Crescent, there was a short path to a playing field with swings, a slide and a roundabout (the teapot lid). Even as quite young children, we were allowed to go up there to play without an adult. It was felt that there would be safety in numbers and the eldest was always in charge. One day we had a fright. An Alsatian dog came and grabbed the scarf that a younger boy was wearing, dragging him round by it until our screams brought out an adult from a nearby house to sort out the dog.

Occasionally, I would go with friends to the baths at the end of Central Avenue. I found the whole experience very unpleasant. The water was always freezing, I could not swim, I had a swimsuit that I hated and I did not like getting my face or hair wet. The hot Bovril afterwards was the final insult. How anyone could drink this dark brown salty liquid was beyond me. As I got older, I learned that you did not have to go everywhere or do everything.

One of my favourite pastimes was playing on my scooter, when scooters had no brakes. The scooter and I were inseparable for years. I cleaned it and painted it. I went to the shops on it. I would have gone to school on it if I could have. I was spotted wearing out one shoe more than the other and then learned to ride it by pushing off either foot in case I was banned from using it.

When I was about 10 years of age, there was a knock on the door one night. My brother answered it and had a hushed conversation with the caller. The unknown caller was about to increase my independence. The following morning, my birthday, I had a two-wheeled bike: a red Elswick Escort. It may have been second hand and it was not a Pink Witch, but I loved it. As I became more proficient on the bike, I went further and further afield. I was allowed to ride virtually anywhere – Cowpen Bewley, down Sandy Lane to Wolviston and to the far reaches of other estates, often going off for the whole day armed with a bottle of liquorice water and a sandwich.

Bonfire night was big, although in truth, the build up to it was just as much fun. From October half term, my brother and I and would start collecting wood for the bonfire that nearly everyone seemed to have in their back gardens on 5 November. We would beg old clothes and make a Guy to be used to demand 'a Penny for the Guy'. I spent my pocket money and any odd pennies we did get on fireworks that were then squirreled away in a box under my bed. Each night before sleep I would arrange the fireworks on the linoleum floor, counting up how many I had and how much they were worth. All this data had to be at your fingertips for the daily playground exchange of, 'who's got the most fireworks'. I had good street credibility around this time as my birthday fell in November and I was often given fireworks as birthday presents. Golden and Silver Rain, Catherine Wheels, Roman Candles, Sky Rockets and Sparklers with which to write your name in the air were amongst my favourites. The great day dawned and it was often raining or misty. When I was quite small, the excitement was almost unbearable as I waited for Dad to come home from work to let off the fireworks after tea. I quite often became asthmatic with the combined effects of the excitement and the smoke and ended up watching the fireworks from the back kitchen window. The following day we could squeeze the last bit of entertainment from Guy Fawkes Night by seeing who could find the most spent rocket cases and sticks that had fallen to earth on our route to and from school.

From my early teens, as soon as Wimbledon fortnight began, playing tennis or playing somewhere with a racquet and ball was the thing to do. In those precious summer weeks, I started my homework on the school bus going home and finished it quickly after tea. I hit a tennis ball up against the back wall, hoping not to break a window whilst pretending to be a tennis star of the day: Maria Bueno, Ann Haydon Jones and Billie Jean King. When I had time and the money for the court, I went with friends to John Whitehead Park or to the tennis courts next to the old baths. We walked or went on our bikes and played until it was too dark to see the ball and the park keeper told us to go home.

Life at home

The estate on which we lived was quite modern for the time. The houses had two living rooms, a scullery and pantry downstairs, and three bedrooms and a bathroom upstairs. The scullery had an elderly inefficient gas cooker, a large rectangular white sink, a wooden draining board and a free-standing kitchen cabinet with pale blue cupboards above and below a drop down Formica-covered work surface.

One living room was a dining room with a drop leaf, gate leg table (covered in a balding brown cover to hide the iron scorch mark made by Auntie Vi) and a large sideboard. The other living room contained a green leatherette three-piece suite, a bookcase and a china cabinet displaying items of china and glass that were rarely used and then only with some trepidation. The room tapered off at the back of the house to accommodate the pantry accessed from the scullery on one side and the coalhouse accessed from a door on the path at the rear of the house on the other. I was always slightly puzzled by the fact that the inside coalhouse walls were painted pink.

There were two double bedrooms at the front of the house and my small bedroom at the back of the house. My room was big enough for a single bed, a chest of drawers, a dressing table and a small cupboard. The room was very, very cold in winter as it was positioned part way over an alleyway with nothing beneath to afford any insulation. As the house did not have insulation in the loft either at that time, whatever heat there was went out in all directions. In the winter, there was ice on the inside of the windows and the lino on the floor was freezing to the feet. Fitted carpets did not feature, in fact any carpets we had were large rugs placed strategically over a linoleum floor covering that was cold to the touch. The air and floor temperatures were great incentives to getting dressed quickly once you put your feet out of the bed.

Across the landing from my room, there was a bath and washbasin and an airing cupboard with hot water tank, but no toilet. The toilet was downstairs just outside the back door. It was, technically speaking, classed as an inside lavatory because it was in a porch area with an outer door that was closed and bolted at night during the winter or on nights when it was raining.

You went to the toilet as the last act before going to bed, but, as a child, you also had a chamber pot under the bed in case you wanted to go again during the night. You were not expected to wander around the house once bedtime had arrived. Although the toilet was not quite outside, it could still freeze in very cold weather and temperature-wise it was not a place to linger. The dreaded spiders inhabited crevices in the painted brick walls and they could creep out without you knowing. There was no electric light in there for many years until the 1960s when ICI did some of its mass home improvements. Going to the toilet developed your singing, partly because you wanted to let others know you were there, and partly because you hoped it might deter the wildlife.

Toilet paper defined the times. First, in the early 1950s, when paper was still in short supply after the war, we had squares of newspaper as toilet paper. We cut up pieces of it and hung them by string from a nail at the back of the door. As a signal that better times had arrived, we then had that hard shiny tracing paper stuff on a roll: the sort that had, 'Now wash your hands' printed on every perforated sheet! Finally, and well into the 1960s, the soft tissue material arrived. What bliss! Nevertheless, if Dad did the shopping, he always bought the Izal, hard stuff because it was cheaper, although he gradually succumbed to buying the softer tissue type.

Having a bath and washing your hair was mostly a weekly event in the 1950s and early 60s and certainly not something you did daily. You could not assume that there would be sufficient hot water on tap and bath time therefore took advance planning. The fire was 'banked up' with coal to get the water hot enough during the next hour or so. In our house, you could tell if there was enough hot water because the hot water tank started to rumble as the water reached boiling point. In fact, if the fire was blazing and you did not have a bath at that point, you had to run off some of the water. Left too long, the water took on a reddish colour because it was wearing away the inside of the copper tank. Only years later, with a house of my own, did I realise that hot water should never be allowed to reach boiling point in a hot water tank.

Sundays were a popular choice for bath-time so that you were clean for the start of the school week on Monday. In my teenage years, having a bath helped to pass the boredom of Sunday afternoons. With the benefit of a portable radio, a late Sunday afternoon bath-time could be strung out for an hour or more as you were accompanied by Alan Freeman ('Evening, pop pickers!') and his 'Pick of the Pops'. By the time you emerged after this time, the gloss painted walls and the windows were running with condensation especially in the wintertime when it was so cold outside. Your skin was wrinkled like a prune. If the bathwater had not gone cold by the time 'Pick of the Pops' was over, the first five notes of 'Sing something simple', a popular radio show with the older generation, would trigger a reflex action so powerful that you leapt out of the bath to turn off the radio. At that point, you knew that Sunday evening had truly set in and all that faced you was the prospect of Monday morning and school.

On weekday nights when he got in from work, Dad would remove his cement-covered overalls and donkey jacket in the porch and hang them up on a nail on the back of the toilet door. We would then leave him alone in the scullery to take off his khaki work shirt and work trousers, enabling him to wash at the large sink so that he did not carry dust and dirt throughout the house. Dad dried himself on cotton towels which ICI provided to their workers because of the nature of their work. These towels were white with a green band down the centre bearing the repeated letters ICI in white along the green band.

After washing, he would go upstairs in his underwear, carrying his work trousers, to change into clean clothes for the evening which were invariably grey flannel trousers, shirt (always with his sleeves rolled up) and sleeveless pullover. Once dressed, he then washed out his khaki work shirt and hung it outside on the line. I can remember going out to take in the clothes from the line on a cold day and finding them so frozen stiff that you had to thaw them out before they could be folded. On such days, we used to put the washing to dry on a wooden clotheshorse in front of the fire and had to sit with it steaming in the room as it dried.

We hand washed small things and sent sheets and large items to the laundry. We did not have a washing machine until I was in my teens.

Even then, using the machine was a very lengthy labour intensive process and nothing like today's front loading automatic machines. The machine was basically an electrically heated water tub. You filled it with water by means of a rubber tube stuck onto the tap in the sink. Once the water was in the tub, you added soap powder (brands like Tide, Omo, Rinso or Oxydol were common then) put in your clothes and switched on a large central paddle that swirled the clothes back and forth in the hot water. Estimating when this process had gone on long enough, you took out each garment with a large pair of wooden tongs and fed it through a hand-operated mangle at the back of the machine to squeeze out the soapy water from the clothes. Using the same water, whites were washed first, then coloureds, ending with the darkest and most likely to lose their colour (red and blue). When you had finished, you had to empty the machine via the same rubber pipe back into a bucket before refilling the machine with clean water for the rinsing and more mangling. Usually, it would take several rinses before the clothes were soap free and ready for pegging out on the line.

Jumpers and other woollen items would be hand washed, rinsed and rolled up in a towel to extract the worst of the water before hanging them out to dry. If you got the water too hot for woollens they shrank, and if you left them in the water too long they could grow a couple of sizes. I once knitted myself a yellow jumper with a blue pattern across the bottom. It was loosely knitted on very large needles and big to start with, but the weight of the wool when wet made it reach down to my knees after its first wash!

You could not wash items like trousers or jackets. Mostly these were made of woollen material that was dry clean only. Dry cleaning was carried out only rarely as it was expensive. The blazer and tunic of my school uniform were dry cleaned once a term. My school uniform could look pretty stained and grubby during the times in between.

The house in Stokesley Crescent had fireplaces in the sitting room and the dining room. Upstairs, the main bedroom had an open fireplace and the other front bedroom had a very inefficient gas fire that roared with flames but gave out little heat. Generally speaking, you only had a fire in the bedroom if someone was ill. On weekdays in the winter, when Dad was at work and my brother and I were at school, we would only have both the fires going in the two downstairs rooms in the evening. Leaving an empty house all day with an open fire burning had its own dangers, not to mention the expense.

In the morning, as Tony and I got dressed for school and had our breakfast, we had a paraffin stove ablaze in the dining room. We had two versions of stoves, one like something you would find in a greenhouse or henhouse and later a more modern one with a dome shaped mantle and stainless steel reflector behind the dome. Both were pretty awful contraptions giving out more by way of smell than heat. We bought the paraffin by the gallon from Billingham Motors or from a hardware shop. You took your own metal can for the supplier to fill with their brand of pink paraffin ('Pick PINK Paraffin') or blue ('Boom-boom-boom-boom, Esso Blue!'). The advertisements claimed that pink was best and less odorous, but I do not recall there being a difference in warmth, smell or how long it lasted. It was never long before you had to set off again with the red metal can to buy and carry home another gallon.

My brother or I lit the coal fire in the sitting room when we came in from school. Lighting a coal fire was a craft learned by observing others. First came setting the fire. Carefully ordered, screwed-up newspaper, pieces of chopped firewood, followed by lumps of half-burnt coal from the previous fire were all placed in the grate and then topped off with fresh coal. Second was the igniting, a work of art and sometimes you were luckier than at other times. Having set fire to some of the paper, there was then a process called 'drawing' that was supposed to make it burn better. However, you could end up with a small alternative blaze on your hands that was something of a hazard to self and surroundings. To draw the fire, you would balance a coal shovel vertically up against the fireplace in front of the carefully built pyre and hold against the shovel a double page spread of an old newspaper to create a draught. Look out if you used a paper that someone had not yet read! If things went well, the fire would catch hold and get the coal burning. If it went badly, the paper would set alight and you had to stuff the burning paper into the chimney at the risk that this act would set the chimney alight and bring down a fall of soot into the room.

If Dad did the fire lighting, he really meant business. Not wanting to waste time, he might use fat left over from the cooking to act as a starter on the paper and sticks. If the sticks and paper were damp he might even use small amounts of paraffin soaked onto rags to start things, but woe betide us if we copied him. His fire raising caused the chimney to set alight on more than one occasion. As he set about cleaning up the mess, he would make a virtue out of the tumbling soot by saying the chimney needed cleaning anyway and it saved the expense of the chimney sweep. The coal burning fires made the walls and ceiling and paintwork discolour and decorating had to be done every year or so.

I learnt to wallpaper and paint from working with my godmother. I loved it. In the 1950s and early 60s, wallpaper came in rolls that had to be trimmed on both sides before it could be hung. For nights before the day of the papering, we would sit by the fire carefully unrolling the paper and cutting off the edges from each side of the rolls making sure we did not cut into the pattern or crease the paper as we re-rolled it. I learnt how to measure the length of paper required, how to hang it and trim it to fit and how to make up the Polycell adhesive to stick it on the walls. However, best of all was stripping the previous walls of the paper that had become dirty. The paper had to be soaked with warm water and then stripped using a special tool. I loved it if the paper came off in great sheets as it sometimes did. Underneath the old paper would be several layers of distemper – a water based paint that had been used before and after the Second World War when resources were scarce. Sometimes the plaster on the walls would come away with the old paper and we had to fill the holes with Polyfilla – another art. Painting the wooden window frames inside never really gave a great finish because the frames were pitted with holes from when blackout material had been tacked to the inside of the window during the war.

By the time I was 12, I was wallpapering and painting the rooms in the house and helping Mrs Walker with her decorating. Once, after decorating the sitting room, I marked the new wallpaper with the coal bucket. I made matters worse by trying to wash off the black mark, only to partially remove the pattern. I was so worried that someone would notice that I tried to re-paint the pattern using my paint box. Nobody else noticed.

ICI was probably a good landlord. We would get quite excited every few years at the prospect of the painters coming to our Crescent to paint the outside of the houses. If they were in nearby Weardale Crescent or Wharfedale Crescent, we would try to calculate when they would arrive in Stokesley Crescent. There was, however, no great excitement about the colour that the house would be painted. In the 1950s, there was no choice. The whole of our estate was done in cream and Buckingham Green: cream – for the window frames and door surrounds, and green – for the front and back doors. There was great entertainment one day when a woman living further up the road painted her front door red. The children in the street went to have a look at the door, and hoped, too, that they might catch a glimpse of this local heroine. We never saw her and she was quickly put in her place by the ICI foreman telling her she had to have the door green like everyone else. She painted it red again after they had gone, but ICI had the final say and she had to return to the institutional green that the rest of us had or risk having her tenancy terminated.

Then came the 1960s with increasing liberalisation and maybe the cream and green paint supplies had been exhausted. The word came round that the front doors of the houses were to be painted in several different colours. But, it was not all good news. You still could not choose to have the colour you might have fancied because it was all to be done to a master plan. We waited, speculated and calculated what our colour would be, trying to work out the sequence as the painters made their way along the street. A number of houses in each road had their doors one colour and then there would be a run of something else. Finally, we saw that the front door of our house was to be part of a run of some kind of blue-green colour. We did not mind too much as none of us fancied the brownish red or the pale yellow that were the alternatives.

It must have been about that time when Dad asked me to choose a colour for my bedroom door during a freshen up of the interior. Looking through the paint chart, I really fancied pillar box red. Needless to say, I settled for powder blue.

Another great ICI modernisation programme included having the house rewired and a 13-amp circuit installed with 3-pin sockets in every room. No more five amp, two pin plugs on appliances! We also had the roof insulated to reduce energy loss. The mess made by men crawling through lofts that had not seen disturbance for 30 or so years by anything more than a stray nesting bird was something to behold. The final movement towards the latter half of the 20th century was the installation of modern fireplaces and the fitting of a Parkray fire that burnt coke instead of coal. There was always something wrong with our fire. All the heat went up to the hot water tank which often rumbled ominously, drawing us to the bathroom to either have a bath, or run off some water so that it did not boil. Inside the room, however, we were rather chilly even when the fire was roaring away.

Gardens and gardening

Each house in our terraced row had a small garden in front of the two downstairs windows with a short path in between leading to the front door. There was a bigger garden at the rear reached by an alleyway or passage between pairs of houses. The front gardens of the houses in our street were for flowers and, if you were very garden conscious, a hedge. We had no hedge. Mr and Mrs Walker had hedges in their front and back gardens. As far as I could see, hedges came in one variety: privet. This evergreen undistinguished shrub required a lot of clipping and shaping and then a lot of sweeping up of the clippings. I could see why this would not have appealed to my Dad.

The front garden of my childhood had a series of large stones that marked out the boundary with next door and the pathway to other houses. Small plants called London Pride grew between the stones. Sometimes other things blew in as seeds and grew by accident – what my godmother called Woolworth specials. As I became interested in gardening, I liked to sow seeds and wait for the plants to show up. I recall sowing something red that did not come up, along with white alyssum and blue lobelia. This gardening was my attempt at something very patriotic and park like. Taller perennials like ground lilac and lupins reappeared each year in the soil just in front of the house. A man further along our street, Mr O'Brien, grew flowers for the Annual Billingham Show. He grew dahlias that had the most perfect looking blooms. Much to our fascination, he put paper bags over the flowers some days before the show to protect them from rain or other damage.

Back gardens were places to grow fruit and vegetables to supplement the food shopping. At first, Mam looked after the gardens. In the 50s, our back garden had a pathway made out of broken roof tiles. To the left of the path was a small lawn with blackcurrant and blackberry fruit bushes along the edge by the fence that separated us from number 49 next door.

In the left hand back corner of our back garden, there was a huge elderberry bush that was very overgrown in later years, pushing against the frail rear fence. I think that this fence was made of pitch coated corrugated asbestos sheets – waste, no doubt, from ICI and probably a health hazard to all who handled it. To the right of the path was the shed and a bed in which Mam grew vegetables and rhubarb. After Mam died, one of Dad's workmates dug over the lawn to grow vegetables. Dad and some of his mates would have the occasional blitz at digging over the garden for planting vegetables and he even imported a large greenhouse at one stage, but projects were rarely sustained and pests ate more of the fruits of their labours than we did.

During and after the Second World War, Dad kept rabbits. They were housed in a row of hutches along the path at the back of the house. Mrs Platt at number 53 was always worried that her terrier dog would catch one of the rabbits. She could not have been more mistaken as one of the rabbits bit the dog on the nose when it came sniffing at the cage. The dog ran off home yelping with blood streaming from his face and did not come near again.

I do not think I associated the furry animals in the cages with the meat pies we had for dinner, or with the monstrous white furry gloves my brother and I had that no other child in the street wore. Dad kept fancy breeds like chinchillas because their skins were desirable for coats and the aforementioned gloves. The gloves Tony and I had were stiff and uncomfortable, probably because they had not been well cured.

Immediately outside the back door was a small plot onto which we tipped the ashes from the coal fires. Over the years, this plot became higher and higher – a place of more ash than soil on which little would grow, probably because it was so acidic.

The shed

Between the vegetable patch and the ash tip was the shed. The shed played an important part in our lives. It was a former Anderson shelter made of pitch covered corrugated iron sheets bolted together in a domed shape. The floor of the shed consisted of old railway sleepers laid parallel to the length of the structure into the soil beneath. Inside the shed, the corrugated iron sheets were painted with distemper. The smell of the rotting sleepers and the damp walls all added to the ambience. The shed was built to act as a shelter for the family during the Second World War and to withstand the worst that Hitler's air force could throw at it. The Luftwaffe did not ever test this structure. It remained in the garden forty years after the war ended, slowly deteriorating, and it was still there in 1986 when Dad left Stokesley Crescent to live with me in Wales.

The shed was where we kept our bikes and where we children sheltered from the rain, as we would rarely be allowed into someone's house to play. Children were expected to play outdoors and if the weather was so bad as to warrant going inside, you each went into your own separate homes to do something quiet. This was alright if I had a book to read or some paper on which to write or draw, or else a colouring book to paint, but it was a fate worse than death if it rained for days during the long school holiday times.

When we were quite young and the weather was fine, my brother and I loved to scramble up and sit on the warm black pitch shed roof. We watched the trains go by on the lines behind the nearby prefabricated houses and wrote the train numbers in pencil on the roof.

In inclement weather, the shed was a place of retreat, a world of intrigue, an Aladdin's cave of mysterious objects, metallic and musty smells and wildlife. It was full of old tools and tins containing assorted nails, screws, nuts and bolts that were kept 'just in case'. I think that most of Britain's 500 or more species of spider lived in there, some of them large and particularly leggy, waiting to drop on the human visitors to their private domain.

I did not like being in there alone much and certainly not without the door being open so I could make a dash away from the wildlife. Actually, the door being open was not a great problem. It never shut properly as it did not fit. Being a wooden construction, it was not one of Dad's best efforts. It was made of some waste planks of wood joined by some cross pieces nailed across the back and painted in a rather pleasant pale blue undercoat. It had to fit an arched entrance rather than a normal door shaped hole and was not well finished across the top. If the wind was blowing in the direction of the door, it did not give much protection to the shed contents or its occupants.

We children occasionally had a feast in the shed, bringing food there from our various homes. The food usually consisted of nothing more exotic than biscuits or bread. Once we had some raw potatoes that someone had sneaked from home. We decided to try to cook them in the old ex-hen house cum shed in the garden belonging to the O'Connells who lived across the road. Our efforts using an old paraffin heater were unsuccessful. The potatoes were inedible. They simply got hot and black from the smoke, and so did we. We all smelled of smoke when we went home – something of a giveaway. The smoke brought on an asthma attack and I was banned from going out for several days.

One summer holiday when I was about 10, I formed a skiffle group that met in the shed and sang Lonnie Donegan songs like, 'Puttin' on the style'. I played the washboard using thimbles borrowed from the house. We made maracas out of empty tins part-filled with a bit of rice. But after failing to find an empty tea chest to make a double base, we disbanded the group within a week and moved on to another craze such as digging a hole to Australia in our back garden, hoola-hoop or being Davy Crockett.

For a time, I kept white mice in a cage in the shed. Dad brought the mice home from work. They lived in a plywood cage made very professionally by a mate of Dad's. When I think about it, those mice were probably saved from some experimental death at ICI as they were used to detect gas escapes. I did not really like the mice very much. They did not smell good, I did not like the feel of their little feet on my hands, and I was always afraid they would run off and I would not be able to catch them.

There was great consternation one day when Dad thought he had seen a rat around the shed. I was told to stand well back whilst he and Tony set about tackling the intruder by setting fire to paraffin-soaked rags stuffed in the holes around the base of the shed. I remember that both Dad and Tony wore cycle clips around the bottoms of their trousers, in case the rat ran up their trousers! We did not see the rat again. I would have felt happier if they had caught it, at least then I would have known where it was. Instead, I was even more wary of going into the shed and liked even less the door being shut if I was in there.

Dad's bike was stolen from the shed. This act was a source of great mystery as the bike was by no means new or special. It seemed that everyone had a bike in Billingham in the 1950s – although clearly not quite everyone. At the end of the day shift in ICI, you could not easily cross Central Avenue, the main road from the works, as scores of workers sped down on their way home.

Food, drink and shopping

My brother and I were fortunate that Mam was at home all day when we were young children. We would come home for dinner when we were at primary school. When I say dinner, I mean the meal at midday. We would also eat another meal at teatime when Dad came home.

There was nothing like the choice of food in the 1950s as there is today, but, even in post-war Britain, children had their likes and dislikes. Tony's and my favourites did not always coincide and Mam did her best to keep the peace. This meant having Tony's favourite on one day and mine on another. Nevertheless, we had to eat what was put in front of us regardless of whether or not it was a favourite.

Two foods that I recall we had alternately were types of peas and milk puddings. I preferred dried peas that had to be soaked overnight with a large white tablet of bicarbonate of soda, before boiling them for a long time. If they were not boiled long enough, they were hard and if they were boiled for a long time, they became mushy. Tony preferred tinned or processed peas. These were either an abnormally bright green colour or olive green depending on the make. They tasted quite different from dried peas. For a brief spell in the summer we would have fresh peas which tasted like another thing altogether. Many of these fresh peas never made it to the cooking pan because we ate them as we podded them.

The milk puddings were made in the oven in blue enamel tins. Tony liked rice and I preferred sago. The best bit of the puddings was the brown caramelised skin on the top and the big treat was being allowed to scrape the tins clean before they were washed.

Mam made all our bread. It was delicious. Auntie Isabel and her husband Uncle Eric talked for years about Mam's bread. They sampled it each day when they came to stay with us around 1953. Mam's cooking repertoire included pastry-based items but not usually cakes. Pastry favourites of the time were meat or fruit pies (top crust only – held up by a Bakelite pie funnel), and curd tart – a sort of pastry base with a baked-in cottage cheese-like filling containing currants. I remember rabbit pies and, once, a pigeon pie. Dad had 'obtained' the pigeon from somewhere and Mam did the conversion job. I did not like the pigeon, but the rabbit was fine.

Coconut macaroons and jam or lemon curd tarts were the nearest thing to cakes that I remember Mam making. My godmother's house, next door, was the place to go for cake. She always had 'a bit of home-made cake' on offer until she was a very old lady and her sight had deteriorated so much that she could no longer bake.

Fruit and vegetables were very much seasonal and local. No mangoes and avocados brought in from miles away, the only exotic things we had were oranges and bananas. We had oranges mainly around Christmas and I was at least five or six before I tasted a banana when out at tea with a neighbour and her boys. The offending fruit made me sick and I did not eat another until I was nearly 30.

Dad would treat me to strawberries, peaches and, my most favourite, cherries when they were in season. In summer, I looked forward to seeing these things emerge from his khaki haversack or from the large pockets in his donkey jacket in which he put his shopping on the way home from work. Strawberries came in punnets made of woven pieces of wafer-thin wood. When shopping, you got used to avoiding the punnets bearing tell-tale red stains on the boxes because this was a mark of the fruit being overripe and bruised. You bought other fruit by weight and it was given to you in brown paper bags. Wrapping in polythene and plastic containers was unheard of then.

Most of our food came from the shops in the village, or the few shops centred around the railway station. The grocery stores were Bowman's on The Green, the Meadow Dairy in Station Road and the Co-op stores – one near the station and the other at the far side of The Green. People would go to the grocer with their order written out on a piece of paper. The order detailed a list of things and quantities that were strictly needed – no speculative or impulse purchases.

The list was handed to the shopkeeper when your turn came to be served and you would watch while your order was made up and packed. All of the prices of the goods were written on your order and you were

Billingham, Station Road.

expected to check that you had not been short-changed before leaving the store.

Butter or lard was cut from a large block and was weighed and wrapped in greaseproof paper. Bacon, with the rind still on, was sliced to the thickness you wanted on a bacon slicer in front of you and then carefully wrapped in greaseproof paper. Dry foods, like sugar, tea, split peas and pearl barley were weighed into special bags and each neatly folded at the top to seal in the goods. Sugar was wrapped in dark blue sugar paper bags and other dry goods in bags with a clear window in the front of the bag to show what was contained within. Biscuits were weighed out of a large tin into white paper bags. You were under strict instructions to watch carefully to make sure you were not being given broken ones. You could buy broken ones cheaply in the market in Stockton but the proper grocers were not keen to give the impression that they ever broke any. You took home your shopping in your own bags not plastic carrier bags. Some people, not us, had their groceries delivered by a boy on a bike with a large basket attached in front. This seemed very posh.

The most common home delivery of all was the milk. Nobody bought milk from shops unless you had seriously underestimated how many pints you would need for the day. The milkman also sold orange juice. Milk and orange juice were brought to the door daily in glass bottles with metal foil tops. Before the era of sell-by dates, the foil tops had a number of raised dots on them to show which day of the week the milk had been bottled so you used them up in the right order.

If the milkman arrived after my brother and I left for school, a neighbour would take in the milk to keep it somewhere cool. Even in the cold weather, it was important that it did not sit out all day as birds would peck off the shiny foil and drink the cream, leaving behind germs that could cause serious illness. If it was very cold, the milk would freeze and the expanding fluid would burst through the foil top.

Our milk was delivered by the Co-op using an electrically powered milk float. We bought coloured plastic tokens from the Co-op store which were each worth a pint of milk. Before you went to bed, you left out a token along with the rinsed empty bottles, one token for each pint you wanted the following morning. The colour of the tokens changed if the price per pint went up. If you had old tokens, you had to put out pennies to make up the difference. One time, there was a mystery in the street. Our milk tokens were disappearing from our doorstep before the deliveryman arrived. Keen to work out what was happening, Dad got up very early one morning to watch through the curtains. At around 5.30 am a woman from another part of the estate appeared and gathered up the tokens from the doorsteps. Imagine her shock when, as she bent down to pick up our tokens, Dad opened the door and confronted her. She claimed she was hard up but we did not have the problem again.

We had some other things delivered. To be more correct, there were some items that you could buy from vans that came around the streets.

We bought tea from the Ringtons' tea van. The tea was already packed in half and one-pound packets with different coloured labels, red, orange, green, blue, each denoting different blends and qualities of teas. The red label was the best. We had the green label. Each packet had stamps on the front of the label. You cut out the stamps and stuck them onto a savings card that was then exchanged when full for money or goods. Woe betide you if you forgot to cut off the stamps before throwing away the packet!

The Sparks Daylight Bakery van from Stockton arrived with bread and cakes on a Saturday morning. My godmother would buy me my favourite chocolate log as a treat. The chocolate log was not so much a log as a small square-ended cylinder about 3 inches long and with a cross section of about an inch and a half. The chocolate was thick, hard and rather lard-like and the chocolate-flavoured cake beneath was filled with buttercream. I savoured every mouthful. First, I would eat the chocolate off the ends, then the sides, and finally the thick stuff off the top and bottom. The cake itself was the last to go. Sometimes, I would have a jelly in a small, waxed case. The thick red jelly covered a sort of pink mousse-like substance that was slightly effervescent. A blob of artificial cream topped the whole thing off. Wonderful! I was in my twenties before I tasted real cream and I was not at all sure about it when I did.

On Fridays, lemonade was delivered in crates that jostled along on the back of a lorry. Fentiman's is the name that rings a bell. No good coming earlier in the week with such frivolities, as payday was not until Thursday. But there was great excitement when the pop man did call. There was so much to choose from. There were large stone jars of ginger beer, bright (far too bright, thinking back on it) green bottles of limeade, and dandelion and burdock, a dark brown fluid that tasted – well – of dandelion and burdock presumably. Later, came Jusoda, an orange fizzy drink and Tizer – bright red with fluorescent overtones, tasting of what exactly I am not sure, but so fizzy it made your head and nose ache.

After the contents had disappeared, the empty bottles had to be washed and returned the following week as you had money back on them. At anything up to 3 pennies per bottle, this was a good earner. As a child during the long summer holidays, you could go around the houses asking people if they had any bottles they wanted taking back. Most things that came in glass included a note on the label saying how much you got if you returned the bottle. Even bottles that had Domestos bleach in them could be returned in exchange for pennies. We would take the bottles to the little corner shop in Teesdale Avenue called the Dairy and then spend the money on sweets and ice lollies.

The Dairy sold penny lollies – cylindrical hard ice-lollies made on flat sticks. Some of the sticks were specially marked underneath the lolly. If you handed in a marked stick, you could have a free lolly. We combed the streets looking for special sticks that had been thrown away. Later, we wondered if the sticks from the streets were re-used and gradually the lollies lost their appeal.

Outside the Dairy was the first kind of vending machine I can remember. The red bubble gum machine on a stand was chained to the wall of the shop. There was a separate machine fixed to the wall that sold small packets of white coated chewing gum pieces – PK – in foil and an outer paper sleeve, or Beechnut in small green-waxed packets. I was not supposed to have bubble gum – and did not like it much anyway – but chewing mint gum seemed to be OK as long as I was not caught chewing it with my mouth open, blowing bubbles, or getting it on my clothes or shoes. You had more pieces for your money with Beechnut even though the mint flavour did not last as long. Another attraction with Beechnut was that the machine would intermittently give out a bonus packet. Sometimes, there would be a queue of children waiting to use it. Word had gone round that no one had had a bonus pack for a while and we felt one must surely be due. Every now and then, someone would make the bubble gum machine produce several colourful spheres of gum by putting a piece of card or thick paper in with their penny. However, occasionally the machine had its revenge by taking your money and not delivering the goods. Whether or not you could recoup your money depended on your currency with the shopkeeper, Mr Allen.

A visit to the Co-op was in a league of its own. This was the forerunner of the supermarket, a departmental store with separate sections for foodstuffs and other goods, but with customers able to benefit from membership of the Co-operative Society. The Co-op near the railway station was the nearest to us. It had a grocery, greengrocery, and butchery. My godparents' son, Ken Walker, worked in the butchery department there for a while after leaving school. Their daughter, Margaret, worked for many years in the tobacco kiosk in the Stockton Co-op.

You paid for your goods in the Co-op by going to a separate cash kiosk in the centre of the shop. Going to the Co-op meant one more thing to remember – the dividend number. All these years on and I can still remember ours – 6877. As a member of the Co-op, you benefited from the profit made each year. After each transaction, you had to give the assistant your dividend number and ensure that you were given a small slip of paper (the check) to show how much you had spent. The kiosk was raised above the shop floor and the woman working in the kiosk put your money into a screw-topped cylinder. She then pulled on a lever and the money was sent off across a system of lines to a separate part of the shop. Within a few minutes, your change and the check came back along these same lines.

The little pink checks, with the all-important totals on them were kept

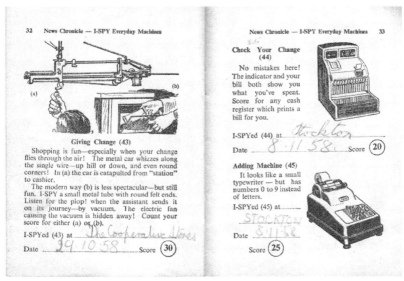

32   News Chronicle — I-SPY Everyday Machines

Giving Change (43)

Shopping is fun—especially when your change flies through the air! The metal car whizzes along the single wire—up hill or down, and even round corners! In (a) the car is catapulted from "station" to cashier.

The modern way (b) is less spectacular—but still fun. I-SPY a small metal tube with round felt ends. Listen for the plop! when the assistant sends it on its journey—by vacuum. The electric fan causing the vacuum is hidden away! Count your score for either (a) or (b).

I-SPYed (43) at _The Co-operative Stores_
Date _29.10.58_ Score (30)

News Chronicle — I-SPY Everyday Machines   33

Check Your Change (44)

No mistakes here! The indicator and your bill both show you what you've spent. Score for any cash register which prints a bill for you.

I-SPYed (44) at _Stockton_
Date _8.11.58_ Score (20)

Adding Machine (45)

It looks like a small typewriter — but has numbers 0 to 9 instead of letters.

I-SPYed (45) at _STOCKTON_
Date _8.11.58_
Score (25)

Pages from I Spy Everyday machines showing the 30 points I scored in the Co-op in Billingham.

in an empty Tate and Lyle syrup tin at home. One night in the year, Dad would sit at the table and get down to the serious business of, 'working out the divi', based on the rate that had been declared for that year. This 'divi' was converted into money that could be spent at the Co-op, or used to pay off your account, or carried forward as savings that earned interest. Sometimes the dividend would be as much as 2 shillings and sixpence in the pound, or 12.5 % – not to be sniffed at.

Meals after Mam died took a different turn. Dad knew how to cook a small range of food and we ate each dish in turn and often. His dishes relied mainly on the 'one-pot' approach. Everything went in to the same pan or pot where it was cooked for hours on end regardless of how long each individual ingredient took to give in.

The everyday cuts of meat we ate were mainly the cheaper but tastier cuts, the sort that might need hours of boiling or stewing to make them edible. Lap of lamb. Brisket. Belly pork. Stewing steak, shin beef and mince. The lamb was sometimes cooked in with the soup. After cooking, the soup was left in a cold place (and there was plenty of choice in our house in the winter) to allow the fat to form a thick crust on top. The fat was then removed before we reheated the stew for consumption.

The lamb fat was often used to make the paper and sticks light the coal fire more easily. Nothing was wasted.

Belly pork was roasted in the oven for hours to remove a lot of the fat. The pork fat was then used for frying other things. At the weekend, Dad cooked the full English breakfast – bacon, mushrooms and fried egg with the bread dipped in the bacon fat. The mushrooms were the large field type that bled black from the spores in the gills and this made the fried egg white look a dirty colour but the taste was good. Dad loved to tell tales of finding huge mushrooms growing locally – one as big as a dustbin lid and routinely they would be the size of dinner plates. You always knew when breakfast was on the go because Dad started singing 'Home on the range'. He always started the song in too low a key and sounded a bit like Lee Marvin. At some point, he had to slide up an octave to manage the song any further.

Another culinary favourite was vegetable soup. Dad would buy bones, usually lamb, from the butchers and boil these up with assorted roughly cut fresh vegetables – usually carrots, turnips (swede) and onions together with a generous quantity of dried vegetables, namely peas, split peas, lentils and pearl barley. This concoction was made in a huge aluminium jam-making pan and there was so much of it that it lasted for at least three days. The first two days the peas and other dried vegetables were hard, as Dad did not seem to know about soaking them and cooking them separately before they were added to the soup. He worked on the principle that they would cook as they soaked up the liquid in the soup. They did, but slowly. By the third day, the soup was quite thick and the peas at last were becoming soft enough to eat.

Sometimes we had sausages, a food that in the 1950s was of very variable quality. Butchers made or lost their name on these items. Sausages could be the repository of things best not talked about, or they could be a product that people would travel miles to buy. In the days before sausages came pre-wrapped in cellophane telling the prospective eater what proportion of lean meat was in the sausage, the banger could hold all sorts of secrets. Some butchers put a lot of rusk or breadcrumbs in with the minced up meat. This must have been where the name banger originated as this type of sausage was apt to burst with a bang when it was being fried. I quite liked these bready sausages as they became crispy after they had burst. Rumour had it that some sausages contained the ground up eyes, ears and tails of pigs and how were we to know?

We frequented three butchers in the village according to the household budget. Sowerby's, owned by the aunt and uncle of Anne Bonson, a close school friend, was noted for high quality meat. Mitchell's was noted for his lovely meat pies and chickens at Christmas. Then there was Dewhurst's, part of a chain of shops whose produce, even to a young and untutored eye, seemed less good than these other places. It sold a lot of deep frozen New Zealand lamb that looked as though it had been cut like pieces of wood with a saw whilst frozen.

One day, Dad arrived home with a pressure cooker that cooked things in minutes that would otherwise take hours to do thereby reducing the amount of gas we used. Having to put a shilling in the gas meter for our supply certainly concentrated the mind on usage.

The pressure cooker and I had an uneasy relationship. I had it drilled into me that unless I put the right weights on the top and put exactly the correct volume of water inside, the whole thing could blow up and scatter our dinner to the four walls. The loud hissing noise the cooker made simply added to its reputation as something that might behave like a bomb instead of a cooking utensil.

Certain foods that Dad cooked I would emphatically not eat. Brawn was one such food. Stop reading now if you are of a nervous disposition. This dish was made from the brains and meat on the head of a sheep or pig. First, find one sheep's head, or half a sheep's head. Butchers would sell these in the days before mad cow disease had spooked everyone about offal and parts of the animal that you do not see pre-packed in a supermarket. The animal's head would be soaked in salty water to cleanse it, and then it was boiled in fresh water for hours. After boiling, the animal's edible bits would be picked off the bones and packed into a small bowl, so much so that the bowl was overfull. The idea then was to place a small plate on top of the meat, adding weights to the plate to compress the contents beneath into a solid mass. The bowl, with plate and weights, was put in a cold place to set. Once set, the brawn could be cut in slices and eaten with pickles or piccalilli. I don't think so.

Another carnivorous delicacy that Dad liked was boiled tripe. Tripe, for the untutored, is the cleaned and bleached muscular lining of a cow's stomach. It was quite a common food in the 1950s and 60s. In Stockton market, there were several stalls that specialised in these less visible or desirable parts of cattle, sheep and pigs. Stalls sold tripe and related products such as udder, chitterlings, cow's heel, and pigs' trotters from large enamel plates and bowls. Round, ruddy-faced women in spotless white overalls and hats would beam down at you from their stalls and serve these pale and jelly-like delights, wrapping the goods you chose first in greaseproof paper and then in sheets of virgin white newsprint to prevent leakage before you got the contents home. Bought by the pound, or piece, these delicacies were either eaten cold or else boiled up with milk and onions before being served with salt, white pepper and vinegar. I could not face trying any of them, but sat and watched my father eat the stuff many times.

Every so often Dad came home from work with fish brought to Billingham by a workmate who lived in Hartlepool. Sometimes it was freshly caught herring and other times haddock. In pre-refrigeration days, I am not sure how the fish kept fresh during the working day. Perhaps he only had the fish during the winter when the air temperatures would have kept the stuff cold enough as it always seemed edible. Dad carried the fish home in his ubiquitous khaki bait bag, a former gas mask bag, in which he took his sandwiches to work.

Dad filleted the herrings and soused them – rolling them up and cooking them in the oven in an enamel dish with vinegar and water. The haddock was usually dusted with flour before being shallow fried until crispy and brown. But, the prize catch was cod's cheeks. If you have ever seen a large cod, you will know that they have huge heads, up to 12 inches across. The cheeks were the sides of the head that would probably otherwise have been thrown away. Perhaps nowadays they end up in fish fingers or other indeterminate products. However, in the days before fish fingers became a staple food, Dad made fish cakes out of these unpromising looking lumps of fish with their gills and fins still attached.

To make the fish cakes, and in line with his 'one pan' cooking method, he would boil up the fish and the peeled potatoes together in a large aluminium saucepan, filling the house with the not-always pleasant aroma of fish being rendered. When the potatoes were soft, he would pour away the cooking water and pick out the bones and bits of skin before mashing the fish and potato together. Rough handfuls of the mashed potato and fish mixture would then be patted into a cake shape, coated with flour and fried in some fat in a frying pan until they were quite dark brown. You learned by trial and error that if you did not cook them to that colour, they were usually cold in the middle. Despite the vigorous pounding with the potato masher at the earlier stage in the production, the flesh of the fish would not easily pass through the holes in the masher and consequently some of the potato stayed in lumps. However, what else was your fork for than to fine mash the potato on your plate? For all the coarseness of the ingredients, they tasted good.

Chicken in the 1950s and early 1960s was still a meat rarely seen other than at Christmas or Easter. We usually had a capon at Christmas – I later learned that this was a castrated chicken. Like eunuchs, the bird became fatter for having its hormones interfered with. I learned that people had a liking for either the drier breast meat or the more succulent leg or wing meat. Dad liked the latter, eating the whole lot, skin and all.

We once had a turkey sent to us for Christmas, but it did not arrive in time. Auntie Vi sent it to us by post from South Wales when she worked for the NAAFI . It was probably Army surplus. Unfortunately, the bird was lost in the Christmas post and turned up oozing from its brown paper wrapping around New Year's Day. The smell was enough to stop a clock. Even now, it affects how I feel about turkey and I still wonder at Auntie Vi's optimism that a turkey would stand the journey in the post without mishap or deterioration.

Christmas day meals went something like this. For breakfast: toast with Tate and Lyle Golden Syrup. Christmas dinner was most often cooked after Mam died by my talented cook of a big brother: chicken, crispy bacon, stuffing made out of pork sausage meat, sage and onion, sprouts, and mashed potato. After dinner, we would have Christmas pudding and white sauce with rum in it. At teatime, I went next door to join my godparents and their family. Someone would knock on the wall at the appointed hour to signal that tea was ready. Tea next door was a revelation. There were sandwiches, tinned fruit and evaporated milk, jelly, butterfly cakes, fairy cakes and Christmas cake with almond icing and royal icing. A veritable tribute to the Bero cook book! I found this meal to be very special, as we did not have tea like this at home.

Singing at the piano with Mr Walker around 1960.
In the foreground are his son Ken and grandson Colin. Note the new TV!

Dad's idea of teatime on Christmas day would be to make a doorstep thick sandwich from the cold chicken and have it with pickled onions and a cup of tea.

Christmas was the only time we had alcohol in the house. We had a bottle of sherry – usually QC British cream sherry, a bottle of port and perhaps a half or a quarter bottle of rum or whisky. Anyone who called over the Christmas and New Year season was offered a drink in the best glasses from this range. Generally, women had a small sherry or a port and lemon (port with lemonade) and men would have a glass of rum or whisky. The drink had to be offered in particular to the 'first foot' on New Year's Day. The 'first foot' was the first person to cross the threshold after midnight on New Year's Eve. For best effect, this 'first foot' had to be a tall dark man carrying a piece of coal to wish the occupants of the house good luck for the New Year. Quite often, this would be my dark haired brother.

The sherry or port could last until next Christmas, but the rum or whisky might go, 'for medicinal purposes' when someone had a cold. I am not sure that it made the cold go, but you certainly fell asleep faster and stopped worrying about your ailment. When I was old enough, I made a Christmas cake to go with the drink. Making a cake with whisky or rum in it seemed a very daring thing to do. We were often still eating the cake well into February, but only with a cup of tea as the time for drinking alcohol at home had long passed for another year.

Eating out

As a young child, eating out was largely confined to having a pot of tea and a toasted teacake in a café in Stockton when I had been shopping with my godmother. Very occasionally, I had fish and chips from the shop in Station Road, Billingham. Chips were sold in three or six old penny (d) bags. The 3d bags were cone shaped and the 6d bags were square. The bags were wrapped around with newspaper to stop the grease from going on your clothes and fingers. Instead, you had printer's ink everywhere. As teenagers, we would buy chips on our way home from the youth club and stop off in the Memorial Gardens to sit on a bench and eat them if they were not already gone by then. Eating in the street, apart from eating fish and chips whilst strolling along the sea front on holiday, was deemed to be rather common.

Around Christmas time, there were chestnut sellers in Stockton. They had portable ovens where the chestnuts were roasted before being sold in small brown paper bags. I liked the thought of the chestnuts but did not particularly like the taste or texture of them.

On the corner of Wellington Street there was a man who sold pikelets (what I know now as crumpets) and muffins from a large basket on the front of his bike. We used to buy pikelets and toast them on a toasting fork in front of the open coal fire before buttering them and maybe putting jam or syrup on them too.

Eating out in a restaurant in the evening was something altogether more sophisticated. It was also not something my father understood. He could not see why anyone would want to go to a restaurant and pay more money to eat there than it would cost you if you cooked it yourself. This approach to eating out stayed with him throughout his life.

My first evening meal out with schoolmates was around the mid-1960s. We were about 16 and trying to make an impression on one another. It was our first Chinese meal. I went with Pam Botcherby, Graham Foster

(Fuzz) and Edward Stanton to a restaurant in Dovecot Street in Stockton that I think was called the Golden Dragon. I had chicken fried rice and prawn crackers and lychees in syrup that must have come out of a tin. As the meal ended, Edward, who was a self-proclaimed communist and therefore had a penchant for all things Russian, decided he would have a Russian tea. The rest of us had already declined the coffee and were ready to go, especially as Edward had to borrow the money for the meal from Fuzz. This 'Russian tea' was just ordinary tea without milk, but it seemed quite exotic as it was served in a glass contained in a metal holder. The tea cost something like a shilling and the rest of us were aghast when Edward paid for his tea and then tipped the waiter sixpence with the money he had borrowed.

Around this time, the Berni Inn made its appearance in Stockton. The Berni was a steak house where the menu was the same no matter where the restaurant was located. You ate, from this menu, steaks of various types and sizes each served with chips and peas with a piece of uncooked tomato on the side. The menu prices started with a 6-ounce rump and worked through price and size increases via sirloin to a 10-ounce T-bone steak, the largest and most expensive of all. After the main course, you could eat the desserts of the time – black forest gateau, apple pie or ice cream. These desserts seemed very exotic indeed to people brought up on milk puddings and school fare like jam roly-poly, spotted dick and treacle sponge and custard. But, the highlight of the Berni experience and the real reason why a teenager found this exciting was the liqueur coffee. This feature of the evening enabled you to drink alcohol before you were 'of age' because this was, after all, just part of the meal. Berni coffee was served sweetened in a tall glass with a measure of the spirit of your choice – whisky (Irish or Gaelic coffee), rum (Jamaican coffee) and so on, topped off with a layer of cream. I did not take sugar in drinks, but quickly learned if you didn't have sugar in the coffee then the cream sank and ruined the experience.

The menu in the Berni later expanded to include something called 'surf and turf' – this consisted of a large piece of battered cod and a steak with all the trimmings. We always looked to see if anyone was gorging himself or herself in this way. Surf and turf was seen as a man's meal and something that certain men ate to impress the women with whom they were eating.

I did not taste Indian food until I was a student in Newcastle. Tony took me to an Indian restaurant in the Bigg Market – all red flock wallpaper and low lighting. These were the days when you showed how cosmopolitan you were by having a very hot curry. The hotter you could stand it, the more experienced you were thought to be at dining out. I actually liked the milder dishes like korma, but did once try a vindaloo curry. A day I was badly sunburnt was probably not the best time to try such a specialist dish.

In Stockton and Billingham, as elsewhere across Britain, there were Italian ice cream and coffee shops. In Stockton there was Pacito's and in Billingham town centre, Rossi's. In these places, the large espresso machine with its steamer for heating the milk signalled a clear and noisy difference between the experience in English tea shops serving pots of tea, instant coffee and toasted teacakes.

As teenagers we would sit and talk for hours in Rossi's and Pacito's over one cup of coffee until we had outstayed our welcome and were shamed into either moving on or buying more drinks. If the café had a jukebox, you could choose a record for 6d and spin out your stay a little longer. If we were well off, we might buy a Neapolitan. This was a small ice cream block consisting of three different flavoured and coloured sections – strawberry, vanilla and pistachio. The three colours were those of the Italian flag.

Radio, music, books and television

Even though television had reached many British homes in the 1950s, I was a radio head. I loved the radio. We had a rented radio from Radio Relay. The house was wired up to receive signals from some transmitter. To this day, I do not know where the transmitter was or how the whole thing worked. You had a speaker housed in a rather smart polished wooden case. The speaker plugged into a small two-point plug on the windowsill in the dining room. From this connection, the speaker could receive four stations – the Home Service (the forerunner of Radio 4), the Light Programme (a precursor to Radio 2), the Third Programme (now Radio 3) and, at night, the exotic Radio Luxemburg. The reception of the broadcasts was very clear, apart from that for Radio Luxemburg. The crackling and intermittent signal of that station added to the mystique of music from abroad that was wild and unforgettable.

As a small child, I loved listening to Children's Favourites on a Saturday morning with Uncle Mac – Derek McCulloch as the presenter. You could request your favourite records and they included such delights as, 'The laughing policeman', 'How much is that doggie in the window?' and 'The happy wanderer'. I also liked Children's Hour on cold afternoons after coming home from school. I liked Derek McCulloch's tremulous voice ('…ooh Mr Mayor, Sir..') as he played the part of Larry the lamb in Toytown, a tale for young children. As I grew older, I enjoyed the serialisation of the Jennings books by Anthony Buckeridge. I recall hiding behind the settee, frightened, listening to Quatermass and being told off for listening to something so unsuitable. I liked the rich, rather refined tones of the actors Peter Coke and Margery Westbury who played Paul Temple and his wife in Francis Durbridge's Paul Temple mysteries.

After my brother had gone off to university, we had a lodger staying with us for a few months to help with the rent. Jack Ramsdale was a kindly bachelor who worked in ICI and had never lived in a place of his own as an adult. Coming out of the army after the war, he had always lived in digs. Jack had a radio that fascinated me. It was a shiny chrome affair housed in a grey-blue leather covered case rather like a tiny suitcase. I was privileged and delighted when he gave me the use of the radio while he stayed with us. I could also play the battery-driven radio in my bedroom choosing the stations I liked on long wave, medium wave and short wave. It was on this radio that I listened under the bedclothes, when I should have been asleep, to the crackles and stutters of Radio Luxemburg, 208 on the medium wave dial, and its endless American pop music. Elvis Presley, Bill Hayley and the Comets and Fats Domino are just a few of the names I remember. Unlike the BBC stations, there were advertisements on Radio Luxemburg. Those of a similar age to me will recall Horace Bachelor's supposed failsafe method (the infra-draw method) for winning money on the weekly football pools. Listeners were advised to send their money to him to an address in a suburb of Bristol that he always spelled out as K_E_Y_N_S_H_A_M, Bristol.

In those days, the football pools were the main means for the working classes to dream of winning a large amount of money. You paid so much for each line of predictions you made about which football teams would have a score draw, no score draw, home win or away win with one another in the matches played the following Saturday. You sent in your predictions either direct through the post or via a collector who received commission on each coupon he forwarded to Littlewoods, Vernons or Zetters. There were tales of collectors who took the stake money and never sent the coupons through. One day coming home from school, I found a bag full of football coupons stuffed in a hedge in Central Avenue. I told my Dad and we reported the matter to the Post Office. It seems a postman had been fed up with his round and decided to ditch the remainders in the hedge before walking off the job.

Dad did the pools, but with no great results. Uncle Eric also did the pools and won enough money (a few hundred pounds) to buy the house they rented and a new car, a little mini Wolsey Hornet. Later he swapped the mini for a bright blue Ford Anglia 105E with its cut back rear window.

Dad also bought the early forerunner of scratch cards each week. You paid to have these so-called football sweep tickets and if your numbers came up you won money. I am not sure how they worked but it involved opening the tickets on Saturday evening once the football results came out and matching your numbers with the pools results.

So important were the football results, that newspapers of the day printed forms for you to write in the football results at teatime on a Saturday. There was hush in the room as Dad copied down the results. As you grew older, you inherited this job. You could tell whether something was to be a home win, away win or draw by the tone and pattern of speech of the announcer. Once copied down, the football pools coupon and the sweep tickets were checked to see if fortunes had been won. If you missed the results, there was a neighbour, Albie Timms, who sold newspapers and he would come round our street on his way home bawling, 'Sports Gazette'. At this sound, Dad would give you money to dash out into the street after Albie to buy a copy of the paper that was always printed on coloured paper to distinguish it from the ordinary Evening Gazette. After we had made all the checks, I remember occasional small wins from the sweep tickets, but not much from the pools. However, the stories in the Sunday papers of people who had won, spent, or lost fortunes kept the dream alive for another week.

During the school holidays I spent a lot of time with my godmother and would listen to 'Workers' playtime' with its vocal and comedy acts, including Eve Boswell and Tony Hancock and 'Have a go' presented by Wilfred and Mabel Pickles. In 'Have a go', people in the audience were invited to tell a tale and then answer some questions. Those so invited were then given the 'kitty' for the day which usually amounted to a couple of pounds and some other items that varied with each programme.

The radio encouraged me to read as I heard stories from books that I then wanted to read. My brother and I would often be found sitting on the local library steps waiting for it to open, especially if we had heard that there were new books coming in. I loved going to the library in Bedale Avenue. I liked the smell of polished wooden floors and furniture. In those days, in a library you were expected to be silent or only talk in hushed tones if you had to speak at all. I loved to be the first to take out a book; in fact, it would often be a temptation to me to take it out if no one else had read it – regardless of who had written it.

Enid Blyton was one of my favourite authors. She is said to have written over 600 books in her lifetime. I liked the Famous Five and the Secret Seven novels but my favourites were the Adventure series – such as The Circus of Adventure and The Sea of Adventure. Later, in more politically correct times, Enid Blyton fell from grace. She was accused of allowing children to escape to places and lives that were not their own. Personally, that is what I liked about them. Some even went so far as to say she was racist, sexist and snobbish. Looking back on the books from today's climate she may well be guilty as charged, but, in the world we inhabited the books she wrote simply appeared to be exciting.

As I grew older, I was allowed to take the bus to Stockton on my own or with school friends on Saturdays. I spent time – often hours – browsing in W H Smith's bookshop looking at paperback books. These affordable books were relatively new in the 60s and Penguin books were constantly bringing out new titles in a collectable numbered series. As I moved from children's books, I worked my way hungrily through The L-Shaped Room, Saturday Night and Sunday Morning, Love on the Dole, and many books by J B Priestley, Evelyn Waugh and Edna O'Brien, some of which were thought shocking at the time. The most shocking of all was D H Lawrence's Lady Chatterley's Lover. I spent weeks eyeing it up before summoning up the courage to buy it when it came out as a Penguin paperback. This was partly because I had to save up for another book so that I could take them both to the counter covering the offending D H Lawrence with the more benign purchase, fooling myself that no one would then notice Lady Chatterley's Lover.

As a child I suffered from asthma and bronchitis. When I was about 12, I was seriously ill in bed for three weeks hardly able to breathe. Dad, thinking I might not be long for this world, went out and bought a television. It arrived later that day in all its second hand glory. Just how it arrived at the house is a mystery to me because once installed it was a three-man job to move it even a couple of inches. It was enormous. I say it, but by 'it' I mean the beautiful polished wood cabinet that housed the TV screen. This huge piece of furniture filled a corner of the front room. The TV screen held within this spectacular piece of furniture was only 9 inches wide.

Watching TV was a novelty in many respects. The instrument with its cathode ray tube and valves had to be switched on to warm up long before you wanted to watch it. Only when it was warm did the black and white picture slowly and magically appear. If you were lucky, the picture was stable – that is it did not disappear round and round into the top of the set or shift crazily in zigzags across the screen. If it did either of these things, you had to adjust knobs at the back called the vertical and horizontal hold controls. We had a sequence of second hand sets at home, which were prone to these problems and were no doubt the reason for the original owner getting rid of the set to my unwary father.

Having appreciated that the 9 inch screen size was somewhat inhibiting to a good TV experience, Dad arrived home triumphant one day with an enormous magnifying glass on a stand. The glass was custom built to sit in front of small screens like ours instantly making it seem twice the size. This was all very well if you were sitting dead straight in front of the screen, but if you were at all at an angle to the screen, everything seemed distorted and unwatchable.

We never had a brilliant television picture as we had a simple indoor aerial housed in the loft. In fact, even on a good day we could only receive BBC as this was at a time when you had to have different aerials for BBC and ITV. The outside TV aerial fixed to the chimney was a bit of a status symbol: as I recall it was a huge H-shaped affair for BBC and a St Andrew's cross-shaped one for ITV.

In these days of hundreds of channels to choose from, it is funny to think that there were only two channels, always assuming you had the right aerials. Not only that but the programmes were not continuous and non-stop television for children was years away. We made do with a few children's programmes like Andy Pandy, Rag, Tag and Bobtail, and Bill and Ben the Flowerpot Men. If you turned on before the day's transmission started, you were greeted with background music and the test card, a still picture of a child surrounded by shapes in shades of grey, or colour if you had a colour TV.

The programmes we were offered seemed to vary little for years. We were amongst millions who watched variety shows like 'The Black and White Minstrel Show' and 'The Billy Cotton Band Show'. If I went next door, I could see ITV's 'Sunday Night at the London Palladium' and watch the stars waving to us from the moving circular stage at the end of the show.

In late 1962, on a Saturday night, satire and alternative humour was born in the form of the controversial, 'That Was The Week That Was' (TWTWTW or TW3). Fronted by David Frost with contributions by singer Millicent Martin, and actors including Lance Percival, Willy Rushton and Frankie Howerd, this show became a must-watch adolescent rebellion programme. Surrounded as we are now with programmes like 'Have I got news for you' and wall-to-wall stand-up comedians, it is hard to imagine the shock caused then by the TW3 lampooning of establishment figures.

Home-grown comedy shows like 'Hancock's half hour' that had started out life on the radio transferred painlessly to TV and gradually, mainly on ITV, we were treated to comedy shows from America such as 'I Love Lucy'. They were different from anything we saw in the studio-recorded shows from the UK because of their canned laughter and odd scene shifts that I later understood coincided with commercial breaks.

By the time I was 16, the BBC had launched 'Top of the Pops' with its weekly dose of chart toppers like Dusty Springfield, The Beatles, The Rolling Stones and Sandi Shaw. Watching this programme was a high spot of my week and I would sing loudly along with the chart toppers of the day, sometimes holding that teenage accessory of a hairbrush microphone.

If you missed any programme then that was that. There were no video or DVD recorders and there was no BBC 3 or ITV 2, 3 or 4 with their themed repeats.

Dad brought home a second hand gramophone, a wind up affair that played the old black shellac records that went round at 78 revolutions per minute. They sounded scratchy and occasionally the needle jumped because of damage to the grooves. The records were also breakable as we found to our cost when someone stood on one and it broke into several irreparable pieces. If the record just had a chip taken out of its edge, some people made them into fruit bowls by warming them and bending them upwards into a rough bowl shape. We had a few 78s ranging far and wide in musical tastes: from Wagner's 'Ride of the Valkyries' to Elvis Presley's 'That's alright Mama' and Fats Domino's 'Blueberry Hill'. Being able to hear these repeatedly was quite a thrill, but it was not long before the lack of choice palled and Dad decided to relegate the gramophone to the shed.

By 1962, we had upgraded to another second hand system, this time an electric portable record player. This wonderful piece of kit was the size of a suitcase. It played not only the shellac 78s, but also a stack of new smaller singles and extended playing records (EPs) that played at 45 revolutions per minute as well as the slower revolving long-playing records (LPs) that had as many as 6 tracks per side. We had arrived in the modern world. Friends came round to see and listen to this masterpiece.

Tony bought jazz records featuring the likes of Satchmo, Wilbur de Paris and Sidney Bechet. He saved up for LPs of Billie Holliday and Mahalia Jackson. No one else had heard of these jazz singers but with so few records in the house, I was word perfect with all the tracks before long. He also bought the odd humorous offering such as those of Stan Frieberg. We learned the comic sequences off by heart much to the annoyance of any adult who had to listen to the repeats.

Having the record player opened up the whole new world of Leslie Brown's Record Shop in Stockton High Street. To my amazement, you could go in there and ask to listen to any record. You went into a booth, put on headphones and could listen to the record before deciding to buy or not. Going to Leslie Brown's quickly became part of the Saturday experience. It was there, in 1962, that I bought my first record. I had saved up so that I could buy an LP, Peggy Lee's 'Bewitching Lee' containing her hit single , 'Fever'. I loved LPs with their glossy covers and nerdy biographical notes full of details about the artiste and the tracks. You could even find the words to the songs on some record sleeves and become word perfect in singing along with the record.

LPs were great status symbols and currency. I recall a girl named Dorothy bringing her latest Beatles' LPs to school to show her envious peers. In my Bob Dylan period, I was followed home one day on the school bus by a boy in my year who presented me with Dylan's latest LP offering before catching two buses all the way back to Hart Village.

A few years later, I was delighted to be given a ticket to see Dylan live in Newcastle provided that I wrote a piece for the Berwick Advertiser on behalf of the journalist friend of a housemate who could not attend.

The piece, shown below, signals my falling out with Bob Dylan as he changed style from folk hero to pepped-up electric guitar man. I sold all my Dylan LPs after that.

Talk of the Pops
by FLIP

THE new-style Bob Dylan, with his five piece backing group, invaded the stage at the packed Odeon Cinema, Newcastle, last Saturday night. Before the group made their Newcastle debut, Dylan, dressed all in black, with a top-heavy head of hair, devoted the first half of his programme in seemingly an attempt at pacifying the more traditional folk lovers with songs accompanied only by his guitar and harmonica.

Such songs as "She Belongs To Me" and two well-known ones "Mr Tambourine Man" and "Its All Over Now Baby Blue" met with appreciation.

The presence of amplifiers and drums on stage showed that there was something more to come and it materialised in the second half in the shape of two electric guitars, drums, a piano and an organ.

All this, plus the guitar carried by Dylan himself, proved too much for his "old style" admirers who showed their disapproval of the modernisation with jeers.

The numbers screamed out above the raucous noise of the group were predominantly ballads from earlier LP's, specially speeded up for the occasion.

Th only number to benefit from this treatment was the non-Dylan composition "Baby Let Me Follow You Down". But a rather nostalgic ballad "One Too Many Mornings" emerged as a load of semi-unintelligible rubbish!

Any pause between songs was soon filled in by a disappointed section of the audience with cries of "Show us what you can do" and "Take some lessons from the Animals". These remarks were for the most part ignored.

His last number, "Like A Rollin' Stone" was greeted with approval but this year's Dylan was far different from last year's performance when the audience refused to let him go off without singing an encore. The general feeling was one of disappointment.

My brief foray into journalism provided in exchange for a ticket to see Bob Dylan.

The cinema

As a 9-12 year old, Saturdays meant The Picture House, Billingham. First, I would go to the children's matinee. Up the steps to the right, pay your 9d at the window, and take your thick, rough, coloured paper ticket to the usherette who stood eagle-eyed, grim faced and cane-bearing. The demeanour of 'She who must be obeyed' was designed to strike fear in the hearts of those who thought they might try to sneak in without paying and it worked. The usherette ceremoniously tore your ticket in half and gave you back one half as proof of purchase. Only then, could you go through the black curtained doors where you were directed to your red velour-covered seat.

The whole place smelled. Actually, it stank. The odour of stale cigarettes, dust and the human detritus that the seats had absorbed over the years hung in the air and transferred itself to you whilst you were there. If it was a wet day, it was even worse as the aroma of damp and not always clean clothes and children overlaid the prevailing smell.

Once inside The Picture House there was an air of expectation and much chatter about the type of films we hoped we would see. Cowboys and Indians, slapstick comedy with the likes of Laurel and Hardy and cartoons were the usual order of the day. As time wore on and the film did not start, the chatter would turn to shouting and stamping of the feet to encourage the projectionist to get a move on. Then the woman with the cane came into her second role as she paced backwards down the aisles, smacking the cane against the end of a row of seats if she thought things were becoming too riotous. She practised this cautionary move, too, on the frequent occasions when the film broke and there was an unplanned and unwelcome interval. To the jeers and stamping feet of the assembled throng, the projectionist repaired the film and sent it on its jerky way, usually missing a bit of a scene in the process.

My favourite films were the Westerns. To get full value from the film, we would act it out with gusto on our way home. We poured out into the daylight after the show was over. Across the road we went, over The Green and then down through the village. Leaping over the rough ground of the bomb site just along from the Black Horse, we would shout and fire our imaginary guns with one hand whilst slapping our backsides with the other hand to speed up the 'horses' we were riding. Our play was even more real when the craze for Davy Crockett hats was at its peak. Going to the pictures with your Davy Crockett hat on was simply the best.

On a good day, I would be back at the Picture House a few hours later. This time I would be with my Dad and a packet of Butterkist popcorn for the early show in the evening. Going 'early doors' meant he could walk home with me and then go back for a pint or two in the Social Club by 9.00 pm. Dad seemed to sleep through many of the films. I think he had seen many of them before. He quite liked 'horse opera' as he called the Westerns. The black and white Western films had a formula – fair-haired men wearing light coloured shirts and hats rode white or pale horses if they were the good guys and dark haired men in dark shirts and hats on black horses were generally up to no good. Round and round the same scenery they rode as most films on a cheap budget were made in a studio rather than on location as they would be nowadays. The big difference between the matinee and the evening performance was the bright red glowing points of lighted cigarettes around the auditorium. As people around you lit up, a pall of smoke drifted mysteriously through the light from the projected film. Your clothes and hair smelled of smoke for the rest of the day even if you were not sitting next to a smoker.

Every small town had at least one cinema. Billingham had its Picture House and nearby Norton had two, The Avenue and The Moderne. I remember the special treats of being taken to both of the Norton cinemas to see amazing, new Technicolor productions like 'High Society' and 'South Pacific' which suddenly transformed the black and white experience into wide screen colour and stereophonic sound. By the late 60s, the Moderne had changed into a nightclub – the Fiesta. The club had well known acts and I went there on separate occasions to see Dusty Springfield and Frankie Howerd.

Stockton had an Odeon that was bigger and smarter than other cinemas and the ABC or Globe that doubled as a theatre and cinema.

My brother and I went to The Globe on the Christmas pantomime visit arranged by ICI for all the children of its employees. We children went in bus loads from Billingham to the pantomime and as part of the treat had free sweets and ice creams. I quite liked the sweets and ice cream but, in truth, I was slightly wary of the pantomime, especially of one of the cast taking you up onto the stage, as seemed to happen if you were near the front or at the ends of the rows. I was fascinated, though, by the principal 'boys' in their fine clothes and by the ugly 'women', never once knowing until I was much older that they were reversed gender roles.

The Beatles came to The Globe in the 60s, 22 November 1963 to be precise, but I did not see them. I did, however, see their first film there, 'A Hard Day's Night'. The Beatles may as well have been there in person because the cinemagoers screamed and shouted every time one of the Fab Four came on screen.

My first date with a boy from school was to the cinema to see 'West Side Story'. The film has such an impression on me that I saw it a further seven times. By the end of the year, my friends and I danced our way through the Memorial Gardens in Station Road each Friday night on our way home from the youth club pretending to be Jets and Sharks and singing our word-perfect renditions of the songs from the show.

Other blockbusters of the early half of the 60s were 'Lawrence of Arabia', and 'My Fair Lady'. Films were classified as U, which meant anyone could see them; A, which meant you had to be accompanied by an adult, i.e. someone of 21 years or more, and X, which meant you could only see it if you were 21 or over.

The club

The club featured large in the lives of working men in the North East. There were several clubs in Billingham each with their own clientele. My father frequented two, The Social Club and the Synthonia Club. The Social Club occupied an old house along Chapel Road just yards away from its neighbours the Billingham Spiritualist Church, a tiny betting shop, Roy's furniture store and the Church of England Infants' school. The Synthonia, on Belasis Avenue, owed its strange sounding name to the synthetic ammonia that was a main part of ICI Billingham's agricultural and chemical production. The Synthonia was for ICI workers and served drinks from late afternoon to catch the thirsty trade making its way home after the day's shift. The club building was modern and had its own sports facilities for the workers and their families long before the era of leisure centres.

In 1958, Synthonia sports field was opened. The use of the ground was not confined to the 15,000 club members and was an indication of how proud ICI was of its community responsibilities. I played tennis at the Synthonia Club on smart red clay courts and it took weeks to get the red clay dust off my white plimsolls.

Clubs were very territorial places and you had to be a member, or else signed in as a guest of a member. To make sure that there were no gate crashers, a committee man would sit at the door and you had to get past him if you wanted to come in or even speak to anyone in there. These places were not called working men's clubs for nothing. Women were only allowed on Saturday or Sunday evening, and then only after being duly signed in and accounted for by the men who had brought them. Dad spent most of his weekday evenings in the Social Club and then visited the Synthonia on a Saturday or a Sunday night when there was dancing, whist, bingo, or star variety acts, such as singers and comedians, supposedly brought in to entertain the women who might be there as guests.

SYNTHONIA
SPORTSFIELD OPENING
by
The Rt. Hon. the Earl of Derby, M.C.
SATURDAY 6th SEPTEMBER, 1958 — 2.15 p.m.

THE BILLINGHAM SYNTHONIA RECREATION CLUB

Mrs Walker would sometimes accompany her husband, Fred, to the Club on a weekend evening, usually in the summer making a gin and orange last her all night.

I experienced the club from both sides of the fence, so to speak. Dad sometimes asked me to go with him when I was old enough to drink alcohol but prior to that, I went to a club one Christmas on the north side of Billingham to raise money for charity by singing carols with a crowd from school. Standing up on the stage, we were given a big introduction, but instead of people being quiet whilst we sang, they carried on as usual with the chatter, the moving back and forth between the tables, the bar and the toilets. But despite this seeming ignorance, there were a few rheumy-eyed souls in the seats in front of us and we went away with a good sum of money from the collection.

Fred and Madge Walker – my godparents at Seaton Carew in 1952.

School

My first school was Billingham South Infants School. I went there aged four in September 1952. Apparently, I was sent to Billingham South because I was able to walk there on my own and only cross one main road. My brother, who by now was going to Grangefield Grammar School for Boys in Stockton, had attended a much smaller place – the Billingham Church of England School on The Green. Why we seem to have had a change of religion in favour of road safety I never quite understood. In any case, the strategy was not entirely successful as, one day, a man riding a bike managed to hit me as I crossed Central Avenue. Just who had the worst eyesight was never clear. All I know is that, whatever injury I had, nothing was worse than having a tear in my new green mackintosh and dreading going home to tell someone.

Billingham South was an all-age school, a so-called modern school built in the 1930s, I think. It was a long building with the hall at the centre and playing fields around one side.

My first teacher was Miss Keep, a short round woman who seemed old but was probably only in her first teaching job. In keeping with the traditions of the time, she smacked me across the fingers one day with a ruler because I did not get all my sums right. I was very wary of her after that.

As very small children, we were expected to put our heads down on the desks in the afternoon and have a nap. There was no way I was going to fall asleep, and especially so after a girl called Margaret was sick on the desk one day after knocking back an extra bottle of lukewarm milk. This made me wary of both school milk and Margaret.

The headmistress was a tiny woman called Miss Ireland (or was it Island?) who wore a red suit with a tight skirt and a short jacket. I was fascinated by the very high heels on her shoes. If you were sent to her room, you had to knock on the door and wait to see which colour light

Little Miss Muffet is the one seated on the chair.
I am sitting at the front left hand side as you look at the picture.

lit up on a panel on the doorframe. If the light was red, you had to wait and if it was green, you could go in.

I was bored in the infants' school. I recall being given cards to read with simple words and phrases on them. I could already read simple books by the time I started school, having been taught and heavily practised on 'The Little Red Hen' by my mother's sister, Auntie Gertie. However, the system could not cope with that and I was given the cards to read like everyone else. I have a photograph of my class in a play about Little Miss Muffet. The little girl in the white clothes in the centre was Miss Muffet but I do not know quite what parts the rest of us played. There was nothing so sophisticated as dramatic costumes. You can see how poorly dressed we were in that post-war era. Nothing matches and some of the children are quite clearly wearing things that were long since worn out, or were too small, or belonged to older siblings or adults. At least, having only an older brother, I was not subject to the ignominy of hand-me-downs.

From the infants' school I progressed to the junior school with a short break for my time in Wales when I was 9 years old. The head of Billingham South Junior School, Dudley Chapman, was a large man with a moustache . He lived in a large house (The Beeches or Holmesdale?) on Station Road.

Mrs Harrison's J4 class around 1958-1959.

Once I came back home to Billingham in 1957, I joined Mrs Harrison's class. She was a farmer's wife from outside Stockton. She took me under her wing rather, taking me to her home for tea a couple of times after which her husband drove me home in their farm Land Rover. Mrs Harrison had a son with special needs who lived away somewhere and only came home very occasionally. Her school reports of me were kindly and encouraging and did a lot to restore my confidence after my brief flirtation with school in Wales.

Class sizes were large. My school report of the time shows that there were 44 in my class and 121 in the year group. Not all could have been present on the day the photograph was taken.

The school was catering for the baby boomers' generation from quite a wide catchment area. I recall children who came from Greatham as well as the surrounding estates in Billingham.

The emphasis was very firmly on English and arithmetic. Although I remember doing other things such as projects with a humanities angle, they were essentially further practice in writing stories or answering comprehension questions. Our work was written in pencil for some things like our 'God's Messengers' project because the booklet was made from poor quality paper on which ink would have blotched. In this booklet, we retold stories we had heard about people including Gladys Aylward, Dr Albert Schweitzer and David Livingstone.

For our best writing books, we used at first a scratchy dip-in pen and later we were allowed to use our own fountain pens. The inkwells were in holes in the wooden desks and were filled up each day by the ink monitor, a job to which I never aspired as I managed to get my hands inky enough just handling the pen whilst writing.

We wrote about things that were seasonal, such as the story of Guy Fawkes around 5 November. Our work was mainly factual or based on books we had read or had read to us. We did dictation where we had to listen to the teacher and write down exactly what she said, including punctuation. We spent hours answering questions to test our comprehension of passages we had read. We learned about opposites, plurals, tenses of verbs, adjectives and pronouns and wrote sentences and short accounts such as, 'Train versus bus' to reveal whether or not we had grasped aspects of grammar and punctuation. The nearest we came to creative writing was to write a story entitled, 'The adventures of a penny' and, 'A conversation between an old boot and an old shoe'.

An extract from my Written English book from 1958, on the next page, gives a flavour of some of the work we did and some insights into how we ensured our gas supply at home.

We had to back all our exercise books to make them stay neat for longer. Any piece of brown paper that came into the house was put away for this purpose. My exercise books were backed, rather inexpertly, in used pieces of brown paper in which our dry cleaning had been returned. Despite using the paper back to front, the fact that it came from the Service Dry Cleaners of 12 Station Road Billingham still showed through for all to see.

We did some practical craft activities. The one that sticks in my mind was knitting. This was for girls only I think and I do not recall what the boys did at that time in the lesson. The task was to knit woollen mittens using 4-ply wool and four needles. I eventually mastered the technique using some wool in a very unlovely shade of green, but I was quite slow at the task. After seeing that others were already on their second pair and I had barely gone beyond the ribbed cuff of one mitten, I offered to take the register to the office and collect all the others on the way. I got away with this ruse for several weeks before Mrs Harrison discovered my ploy. Then, I had to stay in over break times to catch up and complete the

21st January.

Conversation between an Old Boot and an Old Shoe.

It was a cold day in December, and felt like a cup of tea. So I put the kettle on the gas, the gas would not light so I got a shilling and went under the stairs to put the shilling in the gas meter. There on the shelf was an old boot and an old shoe and they were having a conversation.

"Oh dear", said the old boot. "What are you grumbling about now? Your's, You're always grumbling said the old shoe, I was just thinking about the time when I was an army boot. and I was thinking about my twin brother and where he might be", said the boot. "When I was a

offending articles. No one
else in the family was treated
to a pair.

We played netball and
had games in the hall. The
stern looking Miss Knifton
took the girls for netball and
somehow I was in the team
one year.

When the weather was really cold we loved to make slides in the ice on
the playground and nobody stopped us in those days before health and
safety loomed large.

We had occasional trips from junior school to 'places of interest'.
I recall going to Fountains Abbey and to the Lake District on day trips
towards the end of term. On a trip to the Lakes, we went on the boat
across Lake Windermere and I lost my plastic raincoat overboard.
It spoiled the trip as I worried all day about telling my Dad. I do not
know why, because he was never really cross even when I might have
deserved it.

The greatest excitement came in the last year at junior school. There
was to be a school trip to London. This was not to be a day trip but
we were to stay a week in a hotel. I do not know if I really wanted to
go, but having mentioned it to Dad, he said he would like me to go
and so off I went. A coach took us down to London and the coach
driver stayed with us all week to drive us around to the many places in
our full itinerary. We went to the Tower of London, St Paul's Cathedral,
Madame Tussaud's Waxworks, Westminster Abbey, Trafalgar Square,
past Buckingham Palace and so on.

The sights and sounds were so different from Billingham. Big red
buses, black taxis, people shouting as they sold things on street corners.
I had no idea anywhere so big and so busy even existed. In our hotel, we
had the full English breakfast, we were given packed lunches and when we
arrived back in the evening we had a 3-course dinner. The dinners were
a worry to me because we seemed to have tomato soup every evening
as the starter. I loathe tomato soup but, in common with many of my
generation, I was expected to eat everything that was put in front of me.

With the aid of the dry crusty rolls and a glass of water, I managed to gulp down the soup, whilst trying hard not to taste it.

I did not like the coach travel much, the smell of the diesel was rather unpleasant, but also one poor girl was sick every time we got on the bus. She was made to sit at the front but rarely gave the driver any warning before she made him have to get out his bucket and mop once again. It turned out that the girl was not just travelsick but had appendicitis.

I was friends at junior school with a slight girl called Betty who had long fair curly hair. She lived in Rydal Avenue on the other side of Billingham off Mill Lane somewhere near the ICI factory. We played together sometimes at my house and sometimes at her house. We were allowed to play at one another's homes without knowing the parents of the other child and were expected to walk there and back alone, a distance of at least 2 to 3 miles.

One day, my classmates and I sat down under strict conditions (no copying, no questions and no talking) and did some special work in nicely produced booklets the like of which we had never seen before. In fact, we had been practising the kind of arithmetic, English exercises and general knowledge questions that appeared in these booklets for weeks before. Some time later, the head teacher came in and told us that some of us had done something called 'passing the 11 plus'. From the day that I left the junior school and went to grammar school, people were divided into those who had passed the 11 plus and those who had not. I never saw Betty or some other friends again.

At that time, despite its burgeoning population, Billingham had no grammar school. My brother had gone to Grangefield Grammar School for Boys in Stockton and I desperately wanted to go with him to the adjacent girls' school. This was not to be. It was oversubscribed that year with Stocktonians and all the children from Billingham had to go elsewhere. I had a choice of Queen Elizabeth's School for Girls in Stockton (didn't like the navy bowler hats they wore), a school in Middlesbrough that I had never heard of (nasty brown uniform), or Henry Smith School in Hartlepool, 10 miles northeast of Billingham. Going to Middlesbrough, even though it was only three miles away, was like being told you had to go to the other side of the world because it was in a different county on the other side of the river. I knew nothing about

This is a picture from a Christmas card showing an aerial view of the Headland in the 1960s. Above the tennis courts is Henry Smith's School, its playing fields and the adjacent Hartlepool General Hospital.

Henry Smith School, I had never been to Hartlepool and it was furthest away of any of the choices, but it was at least in County Durham.

In the summer before starting at Henry Smith's, Dad received a letter from the school telling him what I had to have by way of school uniform. It was an extraordinary list and very specific. The most specific thing was that you could only buy this kit from one shop in Hartlepool – Mrs Lightfoot's. Lucky for her! This shop was something out of another era. It was dark and smelled slightly damp and of wool and cotton materials that had not yet had their first wash.

Mrs Lightfoot presided over the dark wooden drawers in which lay yellow-white vests of various sizes, navy knickers, fleecy-lined liberty bodices, white blouses, tunics, amber and black ties, brown leather satchels for your books and an order book for Cash's woven nametapes which had to be attached to every item of clothing. I could not imagine an occasion when I would take off my navy blue knickers at school, but those too had to have a nametape sewn in with my full name in the chosen blue italic script.

The uniform was very 'School Friend 1950s', a black V-necked tunic over a white Peter Pan collared blouse that was very short (some said it was deliberately short to prevent the wearing of black skirts instead of the tunic – a privilege reserved for sixth formers) topped off with a black and amber striped tie and an amber sash worn around the waist. The sash had to be tied like a tie and worn hanging down at the back. However, you soon learned to wear it at the side so as to tuck it into your tunic side pocket because otherwise, during Assembly, some wag would tie your sash to the person next to you and then you would get into trouble for messing around. In the summer term, girls in forms 1-5 could wear a yellow and white striped shirtwaister dress and those in the sixth form could wear an open necked white blouse and a black and white large checked skirt.

1963: Form 4 alpha with Mr Grand. The badges many of us are wearing were the Campaign for Nuclear Disarmament (CND) 'Ban the Bomb' badges which seemed to have been allowed in the socialist world of Henry Smith School. Photo copyright Geo. Holdsworth and Son of Hartlepool.

The only things that were not bought from Mrs Lightfoot's emporium were the shoes. The shoes had to be black, leather and sensible. My godmother took me to buy them from Clinkard's shoe shop in Stockton where you had your feet measured on some form of X-ray machine. The black lace-ups were made even more sensible by having so-called segs (metal studs) hammered onto the outer edge of the heels. Dad made this technical adjustment to them to make them last longer as I had a tendency to wear down my heels unevenly. Shoes fitted with segs became embarrassingly loud on hard surfaces and announced your approach. Socks were white, ankle length and gave little protection against the harsh north-easterly wind in winter. Even in the severe snow

Me with a school friend (in our summer uniforms) enjoying ice cream with Margaret (godmother's daughter) outside her new home in Hatfield Road.

and ice of the winter of 1963, we girls had to wear white ankle socks.

When I was in the third form, some older girls staged a protest about the inadequacy of the ankle socks by wearing forbidden knee length white socks to school. Teachers sent them home with instructions that they were to return wearing the regulation ankle socks. Later, the same girls showed immense initiative by getting a television news company to film them walking to school in their knee length socks and rolling the socks down to their ankles before going into school. There was trouble for the girls when the staff found out, but that was the start of our being able to wear thick black tights in winter. Pupil power!

The first hurdle about going to Henry Smith's School was getting there and back. Each day, four double-decker buses ferried pupils from Billingham the 10 or so miles to a red-bricked building near the bracing sea front in Hartlepool. The buses stopped five or six times to pick up as they drove through Billingham. The very first day Dad told me to walk to Dickie Smith's shop, The Green, the starting point of the bus journey and ask for an older girl, Judith Clark, who was the daughter of one of Dad's mates. Thankfully, Judith was looking out for this timid, skinny creature dressed in a pristine and overlarge uniform including a double-breasted, belted navy gabardine mackintosh that I had nearly grown in to four years later. For the uninitiated, gabardine is a water-repellent chino-style material universally used for raincoats in the first half of the 20th century.

The bus was a bit of an ordeal. I often felt travel sick, especially if

I had to sit on one of the side seats near the open back of the bus. My digestive system did not feel easy travelling at right angles to the direction of the bus. I particularly hated going over the stomach-lurching, hump-backed bridge in Greatham village, but I eventually mastered the art of relaxation as we came up to the bridge.

Some of the double-decker buses used for the school run were very old, noisy, smelt heavily of diesel and had seats upstairs that were in a length of four with a gangway on the offside rather than in the centre of two double seats. I tried to avoid sitting on the inside of one of those long seats, especially as we were often crammed in five or six to a seat. If you had a rowdy crowd of older pupils in the outside seats, they might steal your hat, which you were supposed to wear all the way home, and throw it down the bus. You then had to struggle out of the seat and make your way down the bus to find the hat before the bus prefect lifted her eyes from the erudite book she was usually reading to give you lines for not wearing the hat and for being out of your seat. Despite protestations, it was easier for her to give you the lines than to confront the bullies. Another favourite trick of the bus bullies would be to not to let you out of the seat at your stop on the way home so that you had a longer walk home. I grew wise to this. I would say I was getting off sooner that I actually was and would then wait downstairs until my stop.

I dreaded missing the bus to school because I was not familiar with the route I had to take if I had to catch service buses. I knew that you had to catch one bus to West Hartlepool and then another to Hartlepool, but the mysteries of West Hartlepool bus depot were out of my experience. With this haunting me, I missed the bus only twice in six years at school – once, by accident on the way to school and once by choice when a gang of us decided to walk home at the end of term. Going home was more straightforward and during the O and A level examination periods, I would try to catch a service bus home soon after an exam finished. This was so that I did not have to remain at school and talk about the papers we had just taken in case I discovered that I had made some terrible and irreversible blunder in answering the questions.

During the time when 'Bonanza' (a serialised western) enjoyed its place as a favourite television programme, four of the girls on our bus used to retell the story of life on the Ponderosa in great detail after watching an episode the evening before. Each of the four took on the story from the standpoint of Ben, Adam, Hoss or Little Joe. Doing this filled the journey time and they wrote up the story in their own words in an old exercise book.

Although I did not like the bus, I loved the journey. I liked seeing the countryside in the changing seasons. I loved seeing the lapwings in the open fields around Newton Bewley. Flocks of them would land, take off, and tumble through the air with their beautiful iridescent colours flashing in the sunlight. So impressed was I by the lapwing, that I painted one on the front cover of the nature diary we had to keep as part of form 1 biology lessons. The shape is not bad but the colours in the painting do not do justice to this beautiful and now much rarer bird.

I liked it best when the bus ended its journey by driving along the seafront at Hartlepool instead of going through the town. During late autumn or winter you might see lovely sunrises across the sand and sea or fierce grey tides and skies to match. Sometimes you would see men digging up sea coal that had washed up on the beach, waste from collieries further up the coast. Those for whom it was business had trucks to take away their spoils, but an individual looking to offset the household expenses would precariously balance a wet sack of the stuff on the crossbar of a bike and wheel it home.

There were four classes in our year group – 1 Alpha (ά), 1 A, 1 Beta (β) and 1 B. There were about 35 + children in each class and I was put into 1 Alpha. This was at a time when I had no idea that ά was the first letter of the Greek alphabet and that it was used in such a way that signalled it was better than A.

I found out very much later that in County Durham about 15 % of children passed the 11 plus at that time. This compared very badly with the percentage passing in other parts of the UK and was simply a function of the number of grammar schools available rather than a statement about the quality of intake in County Durham. By way of comparison, some 40+% at that time went to grammar schools in South Wales.

Throughout my time in grammar school, I felt as though I was not very good at anything. My first report from there seemed to endorse that. I was 25th out of 36 in the class and had phrases like, 'Quite good', 'Poor' and 'Weak' for most subjects with the notable (pardon the pun) exception of Music where for some unfathomable reason I had an A – 'Very good'. I can only think that Mr (Isaiah Tobias) Phizackerly either gave everyone an A or else he confused me with someone else.

This first report rather put the wind up me and by the following term, with some expert coaching from my lovely brother, I had moved to 16th place out of 36 and by the one after to 9th. By the time I reached form 4, I was 7th out of 32. I am not sure where the other four pupils went to en route. The assessment processes of the day were arithmetically crude to say the least. Your position in class was simply worked out by taking the percentage mark you had for each subject, adding them all together and dividing by the number of subjects to work out your average and then rank ordering all those in class by their average percentage. This technique also presupposed a level of comparability in subjects, tests set and their marking that would not stand any sort of scrutiny.

Whilst worrying about my own position in the class, it never dawned on me that there were three other classes all deemed to have done worse than I did in the 11 plus. I felt that I was hanging on to being in 1 Alpha by the skin of my teeth. I had to do better. Moreover, with the help of my big brother, I did.

The headmaster was a small man called Wilf Georgeson. He had a little moustache and a deep scar on one of his cheeks. He was not seen

Henry Smith School: Mr Georgeson (centre) and his staff in the 1960s.
Photo copyright Geo. Holdsworth and Son of Hartlepool.

much around school other than when he swept in and out of morning assembly. Rumour had it that he had been a missionary in Africa at some stage in his career. He had a penchant for long prayers and even longer sermons. During these feats of endurance, there would often be some poor soul who would faint or be sick. I do not know which I feared happening around me most, but I quickly had a short list of characters to be avoided in the hall. Neither mishap would put the headmaster off his stroke, and we would have to accommodate the unfortunate individual as best we could by removing the fainted body and making a wide berth around the regurgitation of breakfast, whilst we awaited the end of the prepared holy deliverance.

One day, a group of boys put an alarm clock behind the hot water pipes that circuited the hall. The clock was timed to go off in the middle of the Head's daily sermon. Fortunately or otherwise, depending on your perspective, the boys had not kept their plan secret and I noticed the clock. I moved rapidly along the row so that I would not be closest to it. Word got round and a teacher removed the clock before the alarm went off.

I do not recall having any direct contact with Mr Georgeson other than on the day I decided not to stay on for a third year in the sixth form. Like all other pupils in the alpha stream, I had taken my O levels in the fourth form. So, I had taken my A levels in the year that I was 17 and applied to university. Despite doing as well as I could ever do in chemistry and physics I had blown the pure and applied mathematics. Not having the three A levels all my university offers required, I went back to school for the third year in the sixth form. I had not really understood that the whole idea of the alpha stream was to make sure that you could spend three years in the sixth form boosting your grades, doing the scholarship papers, and then applying for Oxford or Cambridge. So little did I understand this, that I thought Oxbridge was a place.

I found the prospect of staying on another year and doing nothing but mathematics rather daunting. I was advised to start a course in Russian to give me another interest. Within a few weeks, I decided to leave. My brother, who was working in the University of Newcastle after doing his degree there, had made some enquiries on my behalf and suggested that I should apply direct to Newcastle. I did so and was offered a place to do biochemistry but via a four-year course as I had not done any examinations in biology. I was thrilled, but not for long. When I went to see Mr Georgeson to tell him I was leaving, he showed his disdain by sending me off with the blessing that, 'If you will insist on going to some provincial university, so be it.'

The deputy head was a large slow-moving man called Mr Coulson whose disciplinary by-line was, 'Like the Mounties, I always get my man and when I do, I come down on him like a ton of bricks'. The fact that Henry Smith School was coeducational seemed to have passed him by. He was, nevertheless, quite kindly underneath this bluff exterior. He could have become quite cross with me one evening as I dashed for the bus when, as well as pulling my scarf from my locker, out came, and smashed the length of the corridor, a full bottle of whisky. He was quite sympathetic when I told him it was a Christmas present, to which we had all contributed, for our lovely avuncular form teacher, Mr Grand. Dad bought me another bottle to take to school to save my face.

The same Mr Grand was our geography teacher for O level. In his large classroom with big desks for spreading out maps, he instilled in me a fascination for the coded detail in ordnance survey maps of the UK and intrigued me by telling us that a rhinoceros had a brain the size of a broad bean. I cannot look at either a broad bean or a rhino without thinking of this 'fact'.

One teacher who taught me in form 1 was the fair-haired physics teacher, Mr Davis. He had beautiful italic handwriting and told us that he read a page of the dictionary every evening to pick up new words. Armed with my brand new, pocket edition of the Oxford English Dictionary that we had to have with us each day, I tried this myself for a while but fell asleep each evening long before I got even a fraction of the way through the early As.

During a series of English lessons in the first year we were told we were to have speech training. This was an extraordinary experience. The class was lined up facing the walls of the classroom and we were each expected to chant certain specially chosen phrases whilst the teacher (Miss Kirkby, I think) walked around listening in for any lack of Received Pronunciation. 'Henry Higgins hit his horse over the head with a hammer, how awful!' was a favourite that challenged those whose natural inclination was to drop their aitches. 'Come up by bus!' was a quick way of detecting and criticising any Teesside vowels.

Miss Anderson taught us English from the third form until O level. Her nickname was Meg. I am not sure whether these were the initials of her Christian names, or indeed her first name. She was tall, slim, and fittingly dramatic with a talent for reading plays and novels in various voices. We read Mrs Gaskell's 'Cranford' with her in the third form and everyone told us she always got upset about Peter. Pupils before us had woven various tales around why this should be and these passed on from year to year. Miss Anderson came in to the class one day and told us she had chosen the particular books (including 'Richard II' and Tennyson's 'The Coming and Passing of Arthur') we were to do for O level for the confidence-raising reasons that we were not very good and they were easy.

Older pupils told us that Miss Anderson was reputedly diabetic. I am not sure I understood quite what this really meant medically, but we all knew that in practice each mid-morning and mid-afternoon she was sent a cup of tea and a mint Yo-Yo from the home economics department to stop her from fainting. Some child, whose shepherd's pie was probably first in the oven, was dispatched with the refreshments from the young home economics' teacher, Miss Waggett, daughter of the ruddy-faced, twinkly-eyed mathematics' teacher of the same name. The same Miss Waggett, surprisingly to us third formers, later married the bespectacled and ginger-haired Mr (Ding-dong) Bell of the chemistry department.

On receipt of the tea and Yo-Yo, Miss Anderson's teaching would stop whilst we were told rather threateningly to, 'Get on with your work!' After the drinking and eating, there was rather a lot of searching for bits of biscuit in her teeth before normal service was resumed.

Miss Anderson had her favourites. I was not one of them. It seemed that regardless of how well you did your homework, unless you were one of the chosen few, you were destined to get 5 or 6 out of 10 each time. I felt a great sense of injustice in all this and one day checked my homework with one of the favourites to see if my clause analysis was any different from hers. It wasn't, and yet I still got 6 out of 10 – 'Fair', whilst the favourite yet again revelled in 9 out of 10 – 'Very good'. I am afraid that Miss Anderson undermined any respect I might have had for her even further when she told me off for talking in class when it was actually the person in front of me. She moved me to the front of the class and I had a whale of a time with a rather lively character called Carolyn Connor who was also under surveillance. With all the indignation of a 14 year old, I decided from that moment on that if I was going to be blamed for something then I might as well have the pleasure of having done it.

My favourite moment in an English class with Miss Anderson was one afternoon when she was late arriving to the lesson. A lookout had spotted that she was chatting to the suave, suede-shoed Mr Brotherton, another English teacher, some way down the corridor. At a signal to say she was on her way, some wag let off a stink bomb in our classroom. In she came, and at first seemed not to notice, even though the class was dissolving into concealed laughter and choking back coughs. Then she noticed the foul smell of rotten eggs. Looking around at each of us in turn she said, 'Someone's made a smell. Well, you'll all suffer. Close the windows!' With that, she swept out of the room, closing the door after her, leaving us to rush to open windows. She left us there untaught for the rest of the lesson. The offence did not happen again.

How much you enjoy different subjects is influenced very much by the teachers and teaching that you have. I disliked history at school because I was rather afraid of the mercurial behaviour of Mr Wilson (or 'Nodder' as he was known). He had enviable precise and small handwriting, drew the most exquisite chalk drawings of mediaeval villages and heraldic

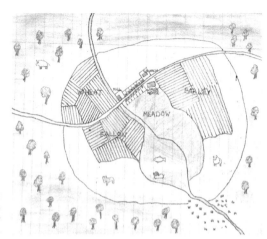

Plan of a mediaeval
village copied from the
blackboard into my history
exercise book in 1960.

devices on the blackboard for us to copy, and dictated, from a hard-backed exercise book, notes that seemed not to vary a word from year to year.

But, as he limped up and down the rows of desks, the sunlight striking his bald pate and his gown floating behind him, he could shoot from calm and benign to outrage in an instant if he found that someone had not copied everything exactly as he expected, right down to underlining words as dictated. One day, he ripped pages from an exercise book belonging to one girl in our class because she had dared to colour in some heraldic shields in the wrong colours. I was very apprehensive of him after that and my grades reflected that rather than a decreasing interest in history.

If I was put off history, I started to enjoy chemistry around year 3 when we had a change of teacher in the form of Miss Doyle (Josie). Miss Doyle was a breath of fresh air. She was young and not long out of university, good-natured and liked by all. She managed us with an easy humour and catch phrases like, 'Isn't chemistry wonderful?' She had a lovely singing voice and played a big part in extra-curricular music and drama. My grades and report comments moved steadily from D, 'Must work harder' with Mr Bell to A, 'Excellent work', with Miss Doyle. My enjoyment of chemistry was a huge influence on my choice of university course.

The chemistry laboratory was old and would have failed instantly any health and safety tests today. During our A level practical examination, an atmosphere of thick white choking fog quickly developed as we each began the set bank of chemical analysis in an open laboratory with inadequate fume extraction. Within an hour, one girl had passed out and was taken to hospital overcome by the combined fumes of ammonia, hydrogen sulphide and sulphur dioxide.

By contrast, the physics laboratory smelled of metals and dry wood. It seemed strangely quiet and sterile in comparison with the smells and potential explosions of the chemistry laboratory. Mr Stockhill's grey lab coat seemed to go well with the tenor of the place. He was quiet and careful in his teaching and I was interested in the subject despite not really understanding a lot of it.

I was taught mathematics by a number of different people. Mr Sanderson, who taught us in the first year, seemed ill at ease with us and who can blame him. He taught us in the gloomy annexe called Morison Hall. This dreadful place, approached up a flight of about ten steps, seemed like an old chapel that had lost its purpose in life. Being some distance down the road from the main school, the indiscipline of large classes of 11-12 year olds did not readily come to ears of senior staff. However, I remember Mr Coulson stepping into deputy head mode pretty smartish when a boy set up the Beano-type prank of balancing a full waste paper bin above the door so that it fell on the hapless Mr Sanderson as he came into the room.

Why I did mathematics at A-level is a bit of a mystery to me except I think there were no other options if you wanted to do science. When I failed to get the required grade at A level, Mr Thompson (Jock) wrote to me saying that he did not understand why I had not done better and that he would welcome me back to join the specialist maths class in the third year sixth. He added with a wink in his writing that it was only my Welsh perverseness that had stopped me from doing better (his wife was Welsh).

I did French from year 1 and then Latin the following year, but only for two years, as we had to choose in year 3 between Latin and physics and history and chemistry. The pairing of things into arts or sciences early on meant that reluctantly Latin had to go although I enjoyed the subject and found the teacher, Mr Holmes, to be such an able and agreeable man. From year 3, and strangely since we had to give up Latin in favour of physics, we were offered the chance to take German. In the 60s, this was seen as a good choice if you were going to do science in the sixth form as so much industrial scientific development was coming out of Germany. Oddly, German was a choice against biology, which was not really regarded as a proper science and was often a subject done by girls who were judged (or judged themselves) not up to the real science of physics and chemistry. I was happy to give up biology and its seemingly endless round of rote learning and precise diagram copying, even down to having to draw a template to make sure we all drew an amoeba in the same way.

The German teacher was a young rather theatrical man called Mr Turnbull (Gordon). He was a great act and, with some admiration from those in his class, took in his stride the fact that he suffered badly from alopecia resulting in large clumps of his auburn hair falling out. Straight from university, Mr Turnbull spent many a lesson regaling us with tales of his student exploits in Germany. He had a class of only eight or so pupils and he would regularly send one of the boys over to the tuck shop to purchase Mars Bars to buy our silence whilst he disappeared to the staff room for a cigarette. We were bribed to say that he had been called away to an urgent telephone message if anyone came asking for him. His favourite tale was of winding up in a strange bed after a night on the town. He had woken in the night with a raging thirst and taken a drink from a glass of water by the bedside only to find in the morning that the glass contained a set of teeth that were not his own.

Being in the alpha stream meant that you did not do any artistic or craft subjects beyond the first year when you had a brief flirtation with art and music. I liked art and longed to be able to draw and paint the dockyard scenes that older pupils did and displayed on the walls, but I do not recall doing anything more than this rather gloomy night painting opposite. I remember Mr White (Chalky) telling me I had done well to include shadows, although he pointed out that they would not go in different directions as I had painted them.

To say that I hated physical education and games lessons at secondary school is an understatement. I did not expect to dislike these lessons. In fact, the many items of precise kit that I had to have for those lessons

quite fascinated me. The navy shorts of a particularly voluminous cut and a rather large size, which would still fit me two years later, the plain white tee shirt, the black plimsolls with brown rubber soles that would not mark the gymnasium floor, were all transported neatly back and forth in a black drawstring bag. And for hockey lessons, there were the additional items of the stocking stitch knitted amber polo-necked jumper, the knitted knee length amber and black striped socks, and the black canvas rubber soled and studded hockey boots. Please note that no tracksuit was allowed. Not even on the most bitterly cold days, when the north-easterly wind blew fit to cut you in two and made your legs so sore that they ached for hours afterwards, could you wear more than the regulation garb described above. The school playing fields were reserved for the boys to play rugby. From late September until March or April, the girls were transported by coach to Grayfields where we were put through our paces on the hockey field in all weathers. If the field was frozen solid or covered in snow so that it was dangerous to play with a hard hockey ball, or impossible to find it in the snow, we were taken to the foreshore to practise stick skills up and down the beach.

The cold air of the north-easterly winds was guaranteed to bring on my asthma in those pre-inhaler days. Many days in winter, I could barely breathe outside in the cold let alone run fast up and down a hockey pitch after a ball. From the outset, I was assessed for hockey as a back or at best (and only when less wheezy characters were absent), a half. This position was further qualified by limiting me to play on the right side of the pitch. The left hand side required far more skill stick-wise than I was capable of mustering whilst breathing at the same time. My reports in the winter months described me as 'Fair' at physical education. In the summer, things were usually far more encouraging ('A great improvement'). No one seemed to notice that in the warm weather I only had to contend with the sport, not with the breathing as well. Summer field sports were focused towards the annual sports day. In summary, I was useless at running but not too bad at throwing things, like the javelin and the discus. One day something happened that can still make me go cold many years later. In the 60s, the technique for throwing the javelin involved running with it underarm and at the last minute bringing it upwards and throwing it. I did this and then watched horrified as the javelin was carried by the wind over the boundary wall on to the footpath leading to the promenade. For a moment, I had visions of some poor soul being skewered whilst out walking the dog. I gingerly climbed up and looked over wall and to my immense relief there was nobody (and no body) there.

The gymnasium came to represent some kind of theatre of humiliation. This was a place where certain flexible and daring individuals could shin up wall bars and ropes like our primate cousins and hang upside down from the same like bats in a cave. I, on the other hand, could not even do a handstand against a wall. I did eventually climb a rope and touch the ceiling, seeing whilst I was up there the grubby fingerprints of endless terrified beings driven up there by the cheap gibes of PE teachers. My legs were chafed and my arms nearly pulled out of their sockets in the attempt. The only thing I really enjoyed in the gym was the termly treat of playing a game called pirates. For this game, we pulled out all the apparatus and coir mats so that they could become islands in the sea of the floor. You were in two teams and members of one chased the members the other as they leapt about and sought sanctuary on one of the apparatus 'islands', before you drowned in the floor 'sea'.

At the end of term, one gym lesson was abandoned and the gymnasium became an assessment centre. Unusually, boys and girls were in the gym together and made to sit on the floor whilst the separate boys' and girls' PE teachers called a register. As they read out your name, you had to stand up. This allowed the PE teachers to remind themselves as to your identity so that each could record the remark and grade that would go on your end of term report. This identity parade was vital because, unless you played in one of the school teams, or you behaved badly, you were pretty well unknown. The reports you had were summary to say the least. There were no records of achievement, or suggestions as to how you might improve your performance in PE or sport. A grade and a comment like 'Fair' were par for the course and almost guaranteed if the teacher did not really know you.

Around Christmas time, the PE teachers came to lessons clad in 'civvies'. That is to say, Mrs Burton exchanged her pleated shorts for a rather tight fitting below-the-knee-length thick plaid skirt with a kick pleat at the back. Somewhat bizarrely, she retained the white polo shirt with the collar up, the white ankle socks, the funnel-necked navy jersey and the plimsolls. And, what did this change in sartorial elegance signal? Why, dancing lessons in readiness for the Christmas party, of course!

Mrs Burton and Mr Allen demonstrated various turns around the floor to the great amusement and some envy of all concerned. With that elegant demonstration as our model, we were then expected to follow suit.

We practised the valeta, the military two step, the waltz, and the Gay Gordons (when nobody knew gay to be anything other than happy) to

School party at Henry Smith's School –
me on left in striped dress next to Judith Clarke.

name but a few, all to the music of an old gramophone and scratchy 78 rpm records.

For the first couple of years at Henry Smith's I had school dinners. Dinners were served in a brick built hut in the yard (the canteen) that performed the rest of the day as a music classroom. On the wall of one of the canteen rooms was a large mural telling the story of how the Hartlepudlians had hanged a monkey during the Napoleonic wars thinking it was a French man washed ashore. If you had a lesson just before lunch, it was generally cut short to make sure that the canteen was ready for the hungry hoards that would queue up ready to eat pretty much anything that was served. Sometimes there were seconds, more often if what was on offer was not so popular.

Regular main course dishes were liver and gravy, mince and carrots, spam fritters and lamb stew. These dishes would be served with mashed potato and a vegetable, often carrots or mashed turnip. Puddings included semolina and jam or prunes, rice pudding, jam roly-poly, spotted dick and treacle sponge. The steamed puddings were always served with custard.

At lunch, we each had the third of a pint of milk that was our entitlement. One day a girl on our table had put salt in my milk and I could not drink it. The prefect on my table said that I should drink it, as it was a waste to leave it. After that, I decided that I would not have school lunches again. I spent my dinner money on some fresh bread rolls and a packet of crisps or nuts from the tuck shop and made crisp or nut sandwiches.

Although Henry Smith's was a co-educational school, and there was no separation of boys and girls in school, there was strict segregation once you went off the premises at lunchtime. The girls were allowed to walk down to one part of the promenade and the boys to another. The same segregation applied to the tuck shops. The girls had access to one shop not far from the school teaching annex of Morison Hall and the boys' tuck shop was opposite the rear gate to the school. In an era before health and safety ruled, we had great freedom to go down to the promenade and play dare games as the high tides came crashing in. We often sat in wet clothes for afternoon school because we had failed to move back fast enough from the crashing waves that came over the promenade railings.

School friends in the yard at Henry Smith's School—note the windows at the back of Hartlepool General Hospital.

In 1963, SCHMAG was born. SCHMAG was the title of the school magazine created by a group of rather creative and somewhat radical sixth formers with the aid of a teacher, Mr Sampson, as censor. Someone carefully typed its 20+ pages onto Xerox skins and then duplicated it onto paper and stapled together with a simple cover. Bold in its articles, it sought to mimic the satirical, sarcastic and sardonic humour that was becoming the flavour of the day on television and radio. I have the first three copies of this tour de force that were published between 1963 and 1965.

There were clubs and societies that we could join at school. I played for the badminton club that a group of us set up. We arranged fixtures ourselves with other schools as it was not really recognised as a sport at school. I asked for a note to be added to my report to boost my sporting profile one year and the teacher wrote that I had represented the school at badminton!

In the sixth form I was the secretary of an earnest little group called the Brus Society which organised debates and guest speakers. I had the job of writing to people to ask them to speak to our society. It took me days to get the protocol right for writing a letter to the House of Commons to someone I was told was an old boy of the school. I had a disappointing reply from The Right Honourable Fred Peart, Minister of Agriculture, Fisheries and Food who sadly was not able to pay us a visit.

December was a busy month for Henry Smith School with speech day, the school play and the carol service. Once a year, on an afternoon in December,

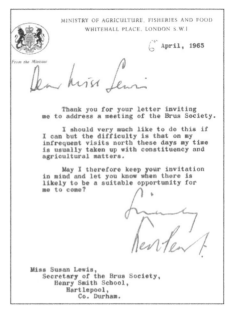

MINISTRY OF AGRICULTURE, FISHERIES AND FOOD
WHITEHALL PLACE, LONDON S.W.1

6 April, 1965

From the Minister

Dear Miss Lewis

    Thank you for your letter inviting me to address a meeting of the Brus Society.

    I should very much like to do this if I can but the difficulty is that on my infrequent visits north these days my time is usually taken up with constituency and agricultural matters.

    May I therefore keep your invitation in mind and let you know when there is likely to be a suitable opportunity for me to come?

Fred Peart

Miss Susan Lewis,
    Secretary of the Brus Society,
      Henry Smith School,
        Hartlepool,
          Co. Durham.

we had speech day in the Borough Hall, Hartlepool. The pattern was similar each year. The chair of governors oversaw proceedings, introducing the headmaster and the guest speaker. Speech day started by the singing of the school hymn ('Our father by whose servants our house was built of old…'). More songs would be rendered by form 1 and then

1965 Henry Smith School science sixth form with Mr Stockhill, physics teacher. I am still surprised at how grown up many of the boys look in this photograph. However, it was hard to look grown up in white ankle socks! Photo copyright Geo. Holdsworth and Son of Hartlepool.

form 2, ('Nymphs and shepherds' made me think too much of Ronald Searle's Molesworth stories to be taken seriously). The headmaster would present his report, the prizes and certificates would be awarded and then the speaker would say a few words. Finally, the head boy would propose a vote of thanks and the head girl would second it. I did not receive a prize for anything until O and A levels. My choice of book for proficiency in O level chemistry (a biography of the male ballet dancer Rudolph Nureyev who had recently defected to the UK) did not go down too well. I had not appreciated that I should have chosen some book to advance my chemistry studies at A level. I learned enough to order a very drab looking but fascinating plant physiology book for my A level prize in anticipation of my university course.

The first school play I remember was Shakespeare's Scottish play. I was very impressed by the witches. One of them, Pamela Botcherby, became a lifelong friend. Pamela was a few years ahead of me at school and lived in the School House on The Green in Billingham. Her parents were the headmaster and teacher in the Church of England school on The Green that my brother had attended.

Later plays were less serious affairs, including 'The happiest days of your life', 'Without the prince', and 'The knight of the burning pestle'. I wonder if any of the casts of these plays went on to have a career in acting.

We had our Christmas Carol Service in St Hilda's Church Hartlepool. Unlike many others who hated attending this event, I loved the occasion. We were all dressed up in our outdoor clothes because it was usually fairly cold in the large church. I was most impressed by the pupils who walked out and up to the lectern and read the lessons. I secretly longed to be able to read one myself but this never happened.

St Hilda's Church, Hartlepool.

Sayings, superstitions and etiquette

Various sayings and superstitions loomed large as I grew up. They revolved around drawing good luck around you and keeping bad luck at bay. One of the first superstitions I became aware of was my mother's dislike of birds in the house. We had nothing so bold as a canary or budgie, but even if wallpaper or curtain material had birds on it, then it was forbidden. A bird in the house brought bad luck. I now know that folklore has it that birds can be a portent of death or misfortune. Auntie Vi bought us some new curtains that bore birds in a repeating pattern through the material. No sooner were they up than they were down once Dad spotted the offending creatures. As Auntie Vi died within two years of her coming up the North East, this only served to reinforce the prejudice against birds.

Along with birds, there were cats. They too were unlucky if they came in the house, or so Mam thought. Dad used to tell a tale of Mam giving what was left of a Sunday joint to a cat once, simply to get it out of the house. But, outside, a black cat crossing your path was seen as lucky and was generally enough for my Dad to have a bet on a horse in the expectation that it (and he) would win. We never knew how many cats had contributed in this fashion, but if Dad ever won anything, he always shared his winnings with those around him. In fact, for years, he and his mate Paddy Jarvis used to have a pact whereby each gave the other a half of all personal winnings, thereby doubling the chances of having something even if it was half one might have had if relying on one's own skill at picking winners.

There were colours that were not seen to be appropriate together, notably blue and green. There was a saying, 'blue and green must never be seen except upon a queen'. I was not really aware of this fashion faux pas until the 1960s when I made an emerald green suit (skirt and jacket) and bought a navy blue shoes and a navy blue blouse from Marks and Spencer's to go with it. I thought this outfit was marvellous, but I also recall being told by my godmother that it did not augur well.

If someone died, then all the curtains in the house were closed until after the funeral. So strongly was this custom observed that you were not allowed to close the curtains until it was dark in case someone thought there had been a death in the family.

When it came to birthdays or Christmas presents, you never gave anyone a present of a knife or scissors or anything with a sharp edge to it unless they gave you a coin, usually a penny, in exchange. This was to 'pay' for the item otherwise the sharp thing would cut the friendship. Dropping knives on the floor was considered bad luck unless you let someone else pick it up for you.

If you dressed yourself by wearing a jumper inside out, you were to leave it like that all day otherwise you would bring bad luck to yourself that day.

You had to avoid numerous other things. Putting a pair of shoes on the table was thought to be a harbinger of at least bad luck and, at worse, death. Friday the 13th was a day to be wary of as it too brought bad things. Walking under a ladder was bad luck and everyone would cross the road to avoid such a fate. Now, I could see some sense in not walking under a ladder because you might bump into the ladder injuring yourself and the person up there. What I did not appreciate was that this belief concerned the Holy Trinity represented by the triangle formed by the ladder against the wall and the disrespect shown as you cut through it if you walked beneath.

But, probably ranking highest in 'things to be avoided' was breaking a mirror. Such a thing was catastrophic, as it would be bound to lead to seven years' bad luck. Alongside breaking mirrors in severity in the bad luck stakes was opening an umbrella indoors. Some people had other umbrella-related concerns, such as not having one as a gift or not picking it up personally if you dropped it, especially if you were a single woman as it meant that you would never marry.

Bad things went in threes, or so I was told. So, if someone close to you died then you cast around to think if there was anyone else you knew who had died in the area who could be added in the list to hasten the achievement of the magic threesome. As we had three deaths in seven years in our house in the 1950s, someone must have smashed a monumental-sized mirror or put a lot of shoes on the table.

The run of threes idea applied to things going wrong or breaking down is probably a superstition I would recall even today when the washing machine had broken down, the TV stopped working and the lock on the gate had seized up. Once you had suffered your three, you might be alright for a while.

I recall proudly learning to whistle around the age of eleven only to be told roundly that 'a whistling woman and a crowing hen bring the devil out of his den'. I was not sure of how this could be, or quite how it would be known, but it made me wary of whistling in the company of adults unless I wanted to be irritating. This saying seems to have a seafaring origin as the whistling was thought to rustle up a storm whilst men were at sea. Mam, coming from Hull, would have been very familiar with the lives of those who went to sea.

There were plenty of sayings and actions that were meant to invoke good fortune. On the first day of each month, you should say, 'White rabbits', as soon as you wake up to make sure the month brings good fortune. On the day of a new moon, you should turn your money over whilst it is your pocket to bring good luck during that month. On New Year's Eve at midnight, you should invite in a tall dark man to be the first into your house in that New Year. The man could be someone who lived at the address but that person had to be outside before the first minute of the New Year arrived. Women and fair-haired people were seen as unlucky to be the first foot, but men with grey hair, which had once been dark, were all right. The first footer arrived carrying a piece of coal for good luck and you would make sure that he went away with a glass of whisky inside him to reinforce the good luck for the year ahead.

Touch wood for good luck. Never step on the cracks in the pavement to avoid bad luck. I devised a game along these lines walking to my primary school. I would only step in the paving stones that had the logo of an S inside a diamond shape in one corner. This was quite tricky as there were not so many of them in some places, so the game had to be amended to be able to walk along the curb stones if you could not see one of the S-pecial stones.

If you spilt salt then you had to throw some of the spillage over your left shoulder for good luck. If a small so-called money spider landed on you, then you took it carefully from you and placed it somewhere where it would be safe. You were never to kill it or break its thread or you would not see the money it had brought with it.

Always get out of bed the same side as you got in otherwise you would have bad luck. See a pin, pick it up, all day long you'll have good luck. This also applied to picking up a coin you might find out on the street. Looking for a four-leafed clover would pass many an hour in a field as these, too, were bringers of good luck.

There were other things that you were told you should not do. 'Never cast a clout until May is out', was one of them. This simply meant, do not change into your summer clothes until the end of May. Frankly, living on the North East coast, you were not inclined to take off your cardigan even in the middle of summer.

Another 'old wives' tale' was not to wash your hair whilst you were menstruating. Quite what this was supposed to do I never did know, but it staggers me to read on the internet that this advice is still being given to women in certain parts of the world, for fear of getting cancer.

Children who had warts on their fingers were said to have acquired the warts through handling eggshells. The only possible factual basis for this if the eggs carried some kind of microorganism from disease carrying hens.

Children were not supposed to interrupt or even necessarily comment on an adult conversation. As a child you heard a great deal that you did not fully understand and it would be years before I understood the full implications of phrases like, 'so and so is 'carrying on' with her down the road's sister in law', and Mrs Smith over the road has had 'everything taken away'. The latter referring to her hysterectomy rather than anything the bailiffs had done.

Getting on a bus, you always waited to let people off before you got on and if there was a shortage of seats, you, as a child, would be expected to sit on your adult companion's knee or stand in the aisle clutching on to the nearest rail and making yourself invisible as people squeezed past.

Going into a shop, you would hold the door open for people to come out before you went in. If a man walked with a woman along a street, he would be expected to walk on the outside. I think that this was so that he, rather than the woman, would catch any spray from passing vehicles. If you crossed over the road, then the man would be expected to take the outside position again. This test was one of a number applied by my father in deciding if any male friend of mine had been properly brought up.

Knowing how to eat with different knives and forks was always a worry, but made easier by the simple rule of working your way in from the cutlery at the outside of a place setting. Eating soup with a soup spoon from the side of the spoon, not the end was the rule, and always holding a soup bowl away from you to eat the last mouthful was an art. To eat pudding you had to remember to do the opposite. I never went anywhere posh enough to have fruit after the meal, thank goodness, as I was concerned to know how to eat some fruits if you could not pick them up and eat them from your hand.

Health

I was born the year before the National Health Service (NHS) came into being. Before the NHS, you had to pay the doctor to come out to see you if you were ill. The figure of 2/6d comes to mind but I must have been told this rather than remember it as, unlike Salvador Dali, I do not remember being in the womb. Although sulphonamides and antibiotics had been discovered, they were not yet commonplace. My brother's godfather, manager of Boots the Chemist in Stockton and a qualified pharmacist, saved my father's life by giving him some sulphonamides when he was very ill with pneumonia.

Many serious viral and bacterial diseases that we take as almost eradicated nowadays were a threat, especially to children. These diseases included poliomyelitis (polio), diphtheria, tuberculosis, smallpox, scarlet fever and measles. Programmes of screening and vaccination for many of these diseases helped to make life safer for those born later but I knew people who had been left partially paralysed by polio or had been very ill because of diphtheria. Measles was regarded as an almost inevitable childhood illness. I had measles and was so ill that the bed was brought downstairs so that I could be monitored closely. The curtains were kept partially closed and brown paper was put around the light in the front room because the disease made me sensitive to the light.

Prescribed medicines were mainly made up from scratch by pharmacists rather than being simply dispensed from pre-packed quantities and strengths. The pharmacist made up things called, The Mixture, The Linctus, The Tablets, The Emulsion and The Ointment in the back room of the pharmacy. You were handed liquid medicines of various colours and aromas in flat-sided returnable bottles stoppered with a cork and packed in a paper bag for privacy. The pharmacist made up the cherry red linctus and brown mixture in clear glass bottles, tablets were held in small black and white lidded boxes and pale green ointment was dispensed in a round waxed box. The linctus was not always as cherry tasting as it was looking and the mixture was best gulped down quickly in the hope that you would be better before the next dose was due. However, the worst of all were the tablets, invariably small, white and inclined to stick in your throat leaving a bitter taste for ages after. All had the GP's illegible handwriting cleverly translated by the pharmacist into your name with accompanying instructions as to how and when to administer the potions.

The two doctors I recall were Dr Woodward and Dr Clouston. Dr Woodward, the senior partner, wore Billy Bunter style round metal framed spectacles and was chauffeured around town on his rounds clad in a morning suit and a bowler hat. He was not liked in our street. Everyone seemed to have a tale to tell to explain their dislike. Dad's was that the bold Dr Woodward had come to see Auntie Gertie when she was very ill. Having examined her, Dr Woodward stood at the end of the bed and told her that she was not long for the scrapheap – not the most distinguished of bedside manners. My recollection of Dr Clouston, a quiet but kindly Scot, was that his hands were always freezing as he tapped your chest and used his equally cold stethoscope to listen to my asthmatic wheezing.

If you went to the doctor's surgery, you turned up and queued with scores of others. The surgery was a basic and uninviting place with linoleum on the floor and painted walls. Many patients would be coughing and sneezing and some would be smoking, making you think that you could come out with more wrong with you than when you went in. All this was long before it was readily accepted that chest conditions and smoking went hand in hand. Some would instantly look a lot better having been in to the doctor and received a sick note to stay away from work. The story always went that Dr Woodward would be writing you a sick note as you went in only stopping when he looked up and saw that he was seeing a child who would not need one.

Having asthma in the pre-Ventolin and steroid inhaler days, meant that I had quite a few weeks off school each year in the winter. The only medicine I was prescribed was ephedrine tablets. These tiny white bitter tasting pills helped you to breathe more easily, but they also seemed to make your heart race and gave you hallucinations as you slept.

The chemist shop also sold some ready-made medicines. Dad's favoured over-the-counter internal medicine for coughs or a cold was Liquefruta. As the name suggests, its basic ingredient was liquorice but it also contained garlic so that you reeked for days after downing it three times a day. For external use only, I had many bottles of camphorated oil rubbed into my chest and back at bedtime to help me breathe better. The strong smell and strange sensation of the cooling and then warming effect of the camphor was very comforting on a cold winter night.

Dad also had some other standbys that were purchased in small brown bottles with an integral dropper. Each bottle was kept inside a sealed cardboard box covered in small print and the signature of the creator of the brew. These potions included Collis Brown's Mixture for diarrhoea. You took a few drops of this magical substance in a glass of water. It contained, amongst other things, morphine and peppermint oil. Another old favourite, which was rubbed on your gums and the inside of your cheeks for mouth ulcers and toothache, was tincture of myrrh. On the principle that if it tasted bad, it must be doing you good, this ranked high up the efficacy charts. I suppose it was marginally better than the cure for toothache followed by one of Dad's younger sisters who swore by rubbing fresh urine (her own) into her gums.

If you were constipated then out came the senna pods to be soaked in warm water before you drank the infusion. Another cure for the same problem was syrup of figs, which also contained senna, but the bitter taste of the senna was disguised by the sweet taste of the syrup. I recall a girl at our school being seen by the nurse because she kept having to leave lessons to go to the toilet. It turned out that her mother gave her a great dose of syrup of figs every morning after breakfast to 'open her bowels'. The substance kicked in around mid-morning causing her some embarrassment.

When I was about 10-11 years old, people thought I was quite underweight (if only they had waited) and I was therefore treated to a regime of malt and cod liver oil. This stuff came in huge round brown jars, rather like enormous Marmite containers. It looked delicious, like molten toffee, as it was spooned out for me to eat. But after the very first taste this illusion was shattered. The taste was execrable and such a conflict with its appearance. I used to try not to smell it or taste it as I gulped it down in one to avoid the disappointment of it not being like caramel. The taste and smell were surpassed only by the awfulness of the neat cod liver oil small children were given as a liquid on a spoon in protection against rickets.

People seemed to suffer a lot from boils – large infected spots which if untreated can cause blood poisoning. If you succumbed to this dreaded pustule, a poultice of hot kaolin was applied to 'draw' the boil and cause it to burst. Kaolin smelled medicinal but looked like rather soft and runny putty. It was heated up and smeared on a piece of lint before being applied hot and bandaged to keep it in place. Your skin throbbed and after a couple of days the poultice would be removed on the assumption that the boil would have burst, often this part hurt a lot as the kaolin had dried and set hard, pulling out any hairs on your skin as it was torn off.

Church and religion

Life around us seemed very simple as far as religion was concerned – you were either Protestant or Catholic. If you were Protestant then you were generally either church or chapel. Both church and chapel featured early in our lives. I do not recall Mam or Dad taking us to church but my brother and I were both baptised in the Church of England, he in Norton Parish Church and me in St Cuthbert's Church in Billingham.

Mam was brought up as a Methodist, being baptised in what was rather scarily described as a Primitive Methodist church. She and her sister Maud had attended Newland Wesleyan Methodist Sunday School in Hull each receiving hymnals for good attendance. Maud's hymnal, received in 1913, had hymns only and Mam's, received in 1916, had words and the music. As a small child, I can remember Mam playing the piano using the music from the hymnal; in particular, 'There is a green hill far away, without a city wall...'. I could not understand why there was such a fuss about a hill not having a city wall, the concept of 'without' in this context being 'without' my experience at that young age.

Dad never went to church willingly all the time I knew him. He said he was made to attend three times a day as a boy and that had put him off forever. He had a healthy disregard for men of the cloth, his cynicism being directly proportional to the level of parsimonious pose they presented. He would rarely attend a funeral, was not keen on church weddings and never, to my knowledge, attended another baptism after those of my brother and me.

So, from this ecumenical background, Tony and I went to Billingham Baptist Church perhaps because it was the nearest place of worship to our home. I must have been about five when we first went and we must have gone for about three years as I have books for good attendance dated 1952 and 1955. I may have gone there willingly at first, but then one Sunday something happened that made me dislike it intensely. When we went in on that day, the floor at the front was opened up to reveal what seemed to me to be a huge pool. During the service people were baptised by total immersion. I found the idea of having to walk into this pool fully clothed in a white robe only to have your head held under the water for what seemed like an age, wholly threatening. I did not want to go back there. I think I thought people were being drowned. I had always been rather frightened of water. Neither my brother nor I learned to swim as youngsters, an adverse reaction to my brother nearly drowning in Billingham Beck aged 6. As a footnote to this experience and having been to the same church since as an adult on other occasions, the baptismal pool area is really quite tiny but it seemed enormous to a small child.

One snowy day, on our way home from Sunday school, Tony and I had great fun making snowballs to throw at one another. When we reached a post box in Lunedale Crescent, the game changed and we threw snowballs at the opening of the box. Suddenly realising what we had done, we ran home quickly and never said a word to anyone, but I often wondered whose letters we ruined when the melted snow made the ink run.

When Mam died, my contact with the church changed. I no longer attended anywhere although I had a brief flirtation with the Baptist church in Llanelli when I lived with Auntie Isabel and Uncle Eric. My elder cousin Heather was in the choir there and we went a couple of times to hear the choir sing and give her moral support.

When I started at Henry Smith's School in Hartlepool, I made friends with other pupils who attended St Cuthbert's Church on a regular basis. Soon, I was going there too. The experience was very different from the non-conformist scene and there was much debate about how 'high' the church was, especially compared with St Aidan's church in the new part of Billingham. Evidence put forth to show that St Cuthbert's was very 'high' was the sacristy lamp that burned in the church and the robes and rituals. I liked the smells and bells. I liked the ancientness of the place and perhaps I liked, too, that Mam and Auntie Vi were buried in the churchyard and I could wander down to the grave and pay my respects before or after the service.

Before long, I was going to the youth club on a Friday night, listening to records on a Dansette record player and playing table tennis and 'hanging out' with friends before trailing home at 9.30 pm calling via the chip shop if we had any money. The great attraction of the youth club was the new young good-looking curate, David Webster. Following his arrival, the attendance rate of young people shot up and we queued up for his confirmation classes.

As confirmation day approached, I had to find a white dress and white shoes. This was another job for my godmother. We traipsed around Stockton shops and the market looking for something suitable that fitted me and was affordable for this one-off occasion. I don't know what I dreaded more, having to wear the dress for the confirmation or being made to wear both shoes and dress for some other occasion to, 'get your wear out of them'. We settled on a 'shirtwaister' (a dress with a shirt like top, full skirt, buttons down the front and a belt around the middle) made out of seersucker and some flat white leather shoes with little holes all over their fronts. I was very conscious that this package cost a lot of money for a single event. The confirmation candidates had to be dressed like brides of Christ. We were relieved to know that the veils were to be supplied by the church.

Confirmation day dawned, 23 March 1962 – a Friday evening to be precise. The Lord Bishop of Jarrow presided and the Vicar Reverend H E Simpson was in attendance. We sat in anticipation in the church, the girls all in white and the boys in dark trousers white shirts and dark ties. I was nervous but the girl behind me must have been more so because all of a sudden she was sick splattering me and two other girls who were sitting in front of her. Someone whisked us out quickly and rather roughly cleaned us up. The offending girl was told off for being sick and we three were made to feel our judgement was somehow flawed for having been in front of her. Back we went to our seats and awaited the holy procession. We had never before seen a bishop complete with his finest vestments, including cope, mitre and crosier.

We each went out in turn for our blessing and to be confirmed. Having to walk up to the altar to be blessed by the bishop was rather nerve wracking and I was conscious too of the vicar hovering nervously. I prayed that the girl would not be sick over him when she went out to receive his blessing. It worked. She wasn't.

We were each presented with a small red prayer book called 'In His

Presence'. We had to write in the front of it, in our best handwriting, our name and, 'Confirmed by the Lord Bishop of Jarrow on Friday March 23rd 1962 in St Cuthbert's Billingham'. Beneath this inscription, the vicar signed his name. The book contained sections on Prayer, the Church, the Holy Communion, the Forgiveness of Sins and the Holy Communion Service. We were tutored in its contents as part of our preparation for confirmation and were advised to keep it with us when we attended communion. I found fascinating the part that explained, with drawings, all the parts of the priest and bishop's vestments and would often peruse these if the sermons were over long or too obscure for mere mortals.

The Church of England suited me. The liturgy was reassuring and the expectations played well with my sense of duty. I enjoyed learning the orders of the different services. Even when I have not been near a church for years, drop me into one of the services and I can still recite the prayers and canticles. I liked the way that you could sit quietly in church and no one would bother you or expect you to socialise with them unless you wanted to. I did not want a church as a social club, but somewhere safe to sit and contemplate on things that were with me or around me in my life.

It was assumed that going to our school you must be a Protestant as there was a Catholic school nearby. I grew up thinking that all Irish and Scots were Catholic as those with Irish or Scots sounding names in our street generally went to the Catholic school.

Story had it that you could not go into a Catholic church if you were not a Catholic. So, I was quite concerned when invited to attend the wedding of my godmother's daughter Margaret to her fiancé, John, a Catholic, in St John's Church, Billingham. I had passed near the church often enough on my way to school, but the inside was a mystery. Going to the wedding then was both exciting and slightly unnerving. I was kitted out in what was known as a nice costume – a pale grey pleated skirt with matching jacket trimmed with dark red velvet collar and red buttons. Accompanying this old-fashioned get-up was a red hat with a tiny artificial flower sprig, sensible lace up shoes and white turned down ankle socks. You would look at this now and think that to dress a child like this was tantamount to child abuse, but this is what the well turned out 10 year old wore in those days. I have the photographic evidence here to show me in my finery, gauchely presenting the happy couple with a lucky silver horseshoe, and remembering to hold it the right way up so the luck did not drain away.

Inside the church, I remember how odd it seemed to see strangers walk in during the service to light a candle and say a prayer, seemingly oblivious that a wedding was taking place.

Presenting Margaret with a lucky horseshoe.

Events and celebrations

The first notable national event and celebration that I can remember was the Queen's Coronation on 2 June 1953. The girls at school were given a pink toothbrush inside a pink plastic beaker bearing the royal crest. We were also given a copy of a book about the new Queen. Tony was at grammar school in 1953 and he was given a more sophisticated book.

To celebrate the Coronation we had a street party in our section of Stokesley Crescent (from about numbers 31 to 75) and all the children dressed up for the occasion. Years later a photograph, sent in to the Evening Gazette by a neighbour, showed us all in our glorious and ingenious get ups. My brother was dressed as Richmal Compton's schoolboy character William from her 'Just William' books. I do not know who I was meant to be, but I was extremely patriotic with a large red, white and blue crepe paper rosette on my head and another even larger one pinned to the front of my dress.

Coronation 1953, street party in Stokesley Crescent, Billingham.

Tony, with his dishevelled cap, dirty face and catapult is second from the right at the back. I am the shy looking one with my tongue sticking out on the far left at the front. I do not recall anything about the party, but I do know that it rained heavily that day and the colours of the crepe paper ran rather badly.

When I was a bit older, we had a few hours off school when the Queen came to Teesside to open something at ICI. I recall standing on a corner waiting for what seemed to be ages and waving a flag as she drove by all too quickly in a large black car. I could not equate the smiling woman in a hat waving with gloved hand with the person wearing full regalia and a crown at her Coronation.

On Friday 22 November 1963, I went with a group of school friends to a lecture about hair, the stuff on our mammalian bodies and not the risqué musical that was to shock people later in the 60s with its full frontal nudity. We had all just entered the sixth form at Henry Smith's and we felt very grown up when one of the teachers gave us tickets to attend this erudite affair. We made the two-bus journey from Billingham into the largely unknown territory of Middlesbrough and the Prissick School base in Marton. I have no recollection of the lecturer and very little memory of the substance of the address, although I was intrigued by the slides that the lecturer used as nothing so modern featured in our lessons at school. As we made our way to catch the bus into Middlesbrough town centre, we were told at the bus stop by a waiting passenger that President Kennedy had been shot.

We were horrified. President Kennedy was such a high profile figure and seemed to offer so much promise to our generation that this news was hard to take in. When we arrived in Middlesbrough, we had to wait for a bus to Billingham and so we went into the nearby Wimpy bar and ate burgers and drank coffee as we discussed what the news might mean. There were many around us who offered their predictions of doom. Some said that it would lead to a Third World War as Russia was bound to be behind Kennedy's assassination. We got on the bus to Billingham, where there was no other topic of conversation. Everyone around us had a view about why he had been shot. People muttered about war, Russia and JFK's stance on civil rights and world peace. It was open season for ardent conspiracy theorists. By the time we had listened to things on the bus journey, none of us seemed very confident about our chances of getting home before a nuclear war started.

At home, Dad already knew the news and we switched on the TV hoping for an update. The assassination dominated broadcasting for days and as the news of Lee Harvey Oswald's arrest came, followed by his death on television, the world seemed a very dangerous place. I remember Mahler being played a lot over those few days.

In January 1965, we heard that Winston Churchill had died. His funeral was probably the first major national event I watched on television. There was a lot of talk and debate about his contribution to Britain during and after the war. Some people said he was a warmonger and others said he was the most important man who had lived in recent years.

Sights, sounds and smells

Some of the greatest defining sights, sounds and smells of my childhood came from the steam trains that ran along the lines not far from our house. I could see the trains from the back bedroom window and hear them anywhere in the house, especially at night if you lay awake. One of our next-door neighbours, Mr Platt, was an engine driver and he would sound his whistle and wave as he passed each day. I imagined him drinking his cold tea that he took to work each day in an empty Gordon's Gin bottle.

As young children, we wandered far further than children would nowadays and one exciting place to go was the railway station, especially when we knew that a large passenger train was due in. We would stand peering through the rails on the wooden bridge over the railway lines, watching people climbing aboard with their luggage while we waited for the engine driver to stoke up the coal fires to generate a large head of steam. The game was to hang on until the whistle blew, the steam exploded noisily out of the valve and the choking yellow sulphurous smoke rose out of the chimney. As this process got underway, a smelly cloud of steam and smoke engulfed the bridge and us and the engine made a juddering sound which signalled it was ready for the off. If we were brave, we stayed put, but more often than not, the terrifying sound of the engine firing up was enough to scare us and send us running off down the wooden steps.

Before the age of day-glow plastic on the sides of emergency vehicles, the sight of a blue light flashing and the sound of a bell ringing were so unusual as to cause curtain twitching, or to bring children and adults out on the street to stand and watch what was going on. Black saloon police cars, white ambulances, and bright red fire engines all with their bells and blue lights fixed on top were a rare enough sight to command points in the sixpenny I Spy books that were popular with children. ICI even had its own ambulances for its workers when anything went wrong, but, sadly, they were not in the I Spy book of Transport.

Cars were a sufficiently unusual sight for them rarely to disturb our street games. Only a couple of our neighbours had a car, one was a brand new pale blue Volkswagen Beetle that Mr Dobson had won. It stood proudly in the turning space by the square and was the object of great curiosity. I was 23 before I had a car of my own (an old Morris Minor that cost £80 and never had all four brakes working at the same time) and I can add up on two hands, and still have spare fingers, the number of times that I had ridden in a car by the time I left home when I was 17.

The presence of ICI in Billingham led to many unusual, and not always pleasant, sights, sounds and smells. The billowing emissions and huge flames from chimneys, pipes and cooling towers were a remarkable sight, especially at night. Sometimes, we would hear a very loud bang or explosion. Dad used to say that this could be caused by hot and cold air or gases meeting and was nothing to worry about. However, if the explosion was sufficiently unusual, nobody would rest until family and neighbours came home after a shift in case there had been a serious accident. Very occasionally, we could smell something like a million rotting fishes or an army of tomcats on the prowl. This must have been some sort of emission from the ammonia plant, perhaps an amine. It was revolting. Washing was quickly brought in from the line and doors and windows closed whilst everyone waited for the wind to change direction and the offending smell to blow away.

This sort of air pollution would be an outrage today, but bad as it could be, people in Billingham had relatively clean air compared with the inhabitants of the nearby hamlets of Haverton Hill and Port Clarence, two places that had grown out of the development of the railway in the 19th century. The area had attracted many Irish, Scots and Welsh people to work in the shipbuilding and chemical industries around the area. Some parts of Haverton Hill were developed as a garden village for the managers of the factories. There were large detached houses with proportionate gardens to grow vegetables and fruit and have space for a lawn and flower borders. However, the very production that the factory managers oversaw led to the rapid decline of Haverton and Port Clarence.

By the mid-60s, the air pollution was such that curtains disintegrated at the windows within months of being there. I delivered the mail there as a holiday job when I was a student. Some days the combining fumes from the sulphuric acid plant and the ammonia plant formed a white acrid tasting choking fog which made your eyes water and filled the air to such an extent that you could barely see houses on the opposite side of the street. The weekly rent for our three bedroomed house in Billingham at that time was 25 shillings (£1.25p), roughly a third of our Dad's weekly earnings. By comparison, the much bigger detached houses in Haverton Hill could be rented for 5 shillings (25p) a week because of the awful conditions that came with the place. By the end of the 1960s, as the Clean Air Act began to bite, most of the housing in Haverton had been razed to the ground.

Going on the dark blue bus from Billingham to Middlesbrough was a rare treat. I liked to sit upstairs as the journey took you very close to part of the ICI works. It was like wandering onto a parallel planet. You passed huge turquoise blue and green lakes. These looked enticing but they were filled with toxic copper waste, copper sulphate and copper nitrate with the orangey-red copper deposited on the sides. Enormous cooling towers loomed large still clad in their wartime green and brown camouflage that had helped to foil the German bombers which regularly tried to seek out the factory during the war. Metal pipe work twisted and turned its way for miles carrying its secret contents to different destinations. Sometimes steam or gas hissed out and unknown liquids dripped at junctions and seams, pervading the air with an indeterminate but very chemical aroma.

The day after the US dropped the atomic bomb on Hiroshima, a manager in ICI sent for Dad and two other welders. Someone escorted the three welders to a part of the factory they had never been before. They were separated from one another and then instructed to use their welding and burning gear to cut up the pipe work in that part of the plant. The pieces of newly cut pipes were loaded onto railway trucks standing nearby and taken away. By the time Dad and his mates had finished, there was no sign of the plant that had existed there. This was the site of the project known as Tube Alloys where it was said that some of the top-secret developmental work had been done for the atomic bomb. I have often wondered if Dad and the other two men had been exposed to any radiation because of the work they did at that time.

We would regularly see the scrap dealers known as rag and bone men touring the streets in a horse and cart yelling their signature, 'Rah, boh, any rah, boh'. Anything they picked up in those days of austerity really had passed its useful life. Clothes would have been patched, darned, let down, taken in and let out to make them last longer or fit other members of a family. Shirt collars and cuffs were turned to extract every bit of wear.

After the rag and bone men had left the street, there was a race to see who could get out first with a bucket and shovel to scoop up the droppings left by the horse. This much-prized stuff went on the garden as fertiliser.

The coal man was a familiar sight carrying sacks of coal or coke around to the backs of the houses to be tipped into the coalhouse. Whoever was in had the job of watching the coalman to see that he delivered exactly the number of bags that had been ordered so that there could be no argument about what should be paid for. These men wore sleeveless leather jackets and caps with flaps at the back to stop the worst of the coal dust from getting to them.

A few days each year, a sea mist descended on Hartlepool, wrapping our school on the Headland in a mysterious blanket. Sounds were magnified in the fog but none more than the intrusive blast of the warning foghorn just a few hundred yards away. You could not hear one another speak whilst this happened.

I discovered late in life, when my sense of smell deteriorated after a viral infection, that I access the world very much through my sense of smell. Babies use their sense of smell to decide what is safe or not. To me it is the most evocative way of recalling things. Certain smells instantly take me to a place or person.

Many smells are redolent of childhood. Sunlight household soap conjures up my godmother doing the washing on a Monday morning. She would rub the collars and cuffs of shirts and the gussets of pants before they went in the tub of the washing machine ensuring that they came out clean and ready for public viewing on the washing line. We used green Fairy household soap or the carbolic-smelling, red Lifebuoy soap in the scullery for washing up, washing clothes and washing hands.

This was the era before the appearance of dedicated cleaning products like washing up liquid or hand washing liquid soaps.

Some days, I would help my godmother to clean her bedrooms. This was an olfactory delight because as I dusted the dressing table and its ornaments, I could sniff the few cosmetics she had – a powder compact, Ponds face cream and, best of all the virtually empty but still fragrant, tiny, flat, sapphire blue bottle of 'Evening in Paris' perfume. The perfume was a floral concoction of bergamot and violets with other notes including jasmine, rose and lilac. She would use a dab of this behind each ear if she was going out anywhere.

Shops in the village had their own smells. The grocer's shop smelled of butter, tea and lard with a dominating note of slightly rancid bacon rind. Greengrocers smelled of cold cabbage. Bakers had a lovely enticing warm smell of freshly baked bread, cakes or pastries depending on the time of day you visited. Butchers' shops had a dull metallic smell of blood. The florist's smelled of chrysanthemums.

Most of all, I liked the smell of the chemist shops in the village. The smell was a curious and heady mix of kaolin and bath cubes – damask rose, lily of the valley and blue hyacinth. Around Christmas, men's toiletries extended the range of smells, when seasonally boxed sets of shaving soap and after-shave appeared. Old Spice in its opaque white bottle adorned with a drawing of a sailing ship was a regular Yuletide purchase for the men in your life. Then, the ingredients of this male and female favourite were legion including smells of oranges, lemons, flowers including carnations, herbs and spices such as sage and cinnamon. It also contained a few compounds that owed more to the chemistry laboratory, such as benzoin and aldehydes.

Deodorants and antiperspirants did not come into their own until well into the 60s. Either people smelled of sweat or of soap depending on the time of day that you met them. Women overlaid their natural body odour with face cream, face powder, perfume or cologne.

One sniff of Pond's face cream, 4711 cologne or Tweed perfume immediately conjures up an olfactory memory of Mam. She had eczema and the very dry skin on her hands had been worsened by using chemicals in the developing process whilst working for a photographer. To help heal her hands and keep them moist, she used a mixture specially made up by the chemist – glycerine and rosewater. This looked and behaved like water. It had to be applied sparingly as it ran everywhere, but as you rubbed it into your hands, it was miraculously absorbed making your hands smooth, soft and slightly cold.

Many men and boys used Brylcreem or Brilliantine on their hair to make it lie down in a slick fashion and shine like a racehorse. These products had a distinctive smell; they also left greasy marks on the backs of chairs and pillows. Many households had anti-macassars, linen or cotton cloths that were draped across the backs of chairs at head height that could be removed and washed so that the hair oil did not damage the chairs.

Our home often smelled of the fuel used to heat the downstairs rooms – paraffin in the morning changing to coal in the evening. There was always a coal dust smell until the fire really got going. To say the coalhouse smelt of coal dust might seem obvious but it is not a smell many under the age of 50 would recognise today.

The smell of mothballs or phenol instantly takes me back to our cold little back bedroom in Stokesley Crescent or, to be more precise, to two large metal cube-shaped biscuit tins that contained our Christmas decorations. In those tins were stored the rolled-up, home-made streamers that Mam had run up on her sewing machine from lengths of crepe paper. The streamers were orange and bright green, the nearest to festive colours she could find in those days of austerity. Also kept in the tins were long since defunct coloured electric bulbs decorated in Chinese lettering that we hung from the Christmas tree by lengths of cotton thread. Just why they all smelled of phenol and mothballs was a bit of mystery, but I once asked Dad and he said it dated back to when he had fumigated the place after Tony and I had had one childhood illness after another.

Holiday times

The first holiday I can remember must have been when I was 5 or 6 years of age. I went with Mam, Dad and brother Tony to a caravan chalet site in Ebberson just outside of Scarborough. We must have travelled by train to Scarborough and then by taxi to the site because I can recall being in a black car.

The chalet was a disaster. The sheets were not clean and outside the next day, Tony saw a rat. That was it, we were back home within 48 hours.

There was no more holidaying with Mam. Most school holidays were spent playing around home. Like others around us, Dad had the Bank Holidays and two weeks in August each year as his annual holiday entitlement. On some fine days, I went to the seaside with my godmother, Mrs Walker, and more rarely I would go with Dad. Mrs Walker and I would make sandwiches and a flask of tea and make the 10 minute walk to Billingham station and catch a train to Seaton Carew some 10 miles away. We would spend a few hours walking along the front, sitting and eating our picnic, spending a shilling's worth of coppers on the slot machines in the arcade and then have a bag of chips before catching the train back in time for Mrs Walker to make Mr Walker's tea.

If Dad took me out, it was a similar sort of routine but the sandwiches were not as good and he usually took me to Redcar. He liked to visit the Zetland lifeboat museum and we would walk along the beach by the tide line. In the summer, Dad would be clad in his dark blue double breasted blazer, wide turn-upped bottomed grey flannel trousers, which flapped over his polished brown toe-capped leather shoes, feet at an angle of 90 degrees. He bought his shoes from ICI – always brown, never black. We beach combed looking for treasure amongst the broken bottles, old rope and seaweed. Our best finds were a half crown (2/6d or 12½ p in today's money) and a fountain pen. Walking along Redcar beach, we would often encounter relics from the war in the form of rusty remains from anti-landing devices and old exploded mines. Very occasionally unexploded bombs were found on the beaches along the North East coast.

Once a year the fair came to Billingham on land next to the old railway station where Allendale Road is now. I went with my godmother. We had candyfloss and toffee apples and rolled pennies down slots to try in vain to win something.

During several of Dad's two-week holidays in August, he and I went down to Llanelli to stay with his sister, Isabel and her family. He usually married his two weeks to the August Bank Holiday that in the early 60s was the first Monday in the month rather the last as it became in 1965. This venture was a major expedition. For days before, we packed all our things into a large expandable mottled grey-blue suitcase, together with things he had set aside as gifts for his sister and her husband. The fare overnight midweek was cheaper than at other times and so we set out to catch the train at 6.50 pm on a Tuesday evening. Dad hated the thought of being late for anything and so we set off 'in plenty of time' for the 10-minute walk at about 6.15 pm. If we were any later, Dad would be in a very bad mood as we struggled round to the station with the loaded suitcase. One year Dad bought a set of tie-on wheels for the case so that he could drag it along a lot more easily, but we still had to allow 'plenty of time'.

The journey to Wales was a great lesson in patience and geography. We had barely boarded the train when 3 miles later we had to change trains in Stockton to catch the Darlington train. From Darlington to York was about 45 to 60 minutes. On York or Leeds station, we invariably had to hang around for hours for a connection to take us across country to Crewe. Dad would have a pint in the station bar while I had lemonade. We then made metal nametapes using a large machine on the

News Chronicle — I-SPY Everyday Machines 19

Weighing Machine (24)
What do I weigh? The machine will tell you—with a pointing finger, a printed ticket, or it may even speak to you!
I-SPYed (24) at ....
LEEDS
Date 26.8.58
Score (15)

Name Machine (25)
Drop in your penny and spell out your name—letter by letter. What fun to see it pressed on a strip of metal!
I-SPYed (25) at ....
LEEDS
Date 26-8-58
Score (25)

station that stamped out letters onto a strip of aluminium. The idea was to fix these strips to your luggage, but I think we made them to amuse me and to pass the time.

Time eventually passed and we boarded the train for the next stage of our journey. Our case heaved onto the rack above the seat, Dad tried to get me to go to sleep as by now it was about midnight or so and we had several more hours on this train. The train was in carriages of separate compartments accessed via corridors along one side. Dad tried to choose a compartment that was empty so that we could use several seats as beds. He would also close the blinds on the corridor side to deter any others from joining us. He left the blinds up on the trackside so that he could see where we were. The train seats smelled stale of smoke and dust. Above the seats were oval mirrors and posters of places to visit and racks like hammocks for your belongings. One time we had just settled in when the door opened and in staggered a very drunk and even smellier tramp clutching a paper parcel of belongings. His odour filled the compartment. I watched him cautiously while Dad chatted to him. He was so drunk that he was soon asleep. At the right moment, Dad pulled down our suitcase and he and I left the compartment for another, leaving our visitor snoring alone.

By 3 o'clock in the morning, we were on the platform in Crewe waiting for the next train to snake its way down through Mid-Wales. This leg of the journey wound slowly through Craven Arms, Knighton, Builth Wells, Llanwrtyd Wells, stopping at every station and hamlet to pick up milk in churns brought by farmers to send down the line in exchange for mail and newspapers dropped off for people in these small places. Strange Welsh voices shouted out greetings and instructions. In the smaller places, the train did not actually stop but slowed down enough for someone to throw out a package of newspapers to land in a net by the line.

From 4.00 am we saw the dawn rise and heard the accents and language change again as we meandered slowly through the rural Mid and South Wales landscape. About 8.45 am we arrived in Pontarddulais, our train journey nearly over. We still had to get to Llanelli and this could be on either another small local train or a bus, whichever came first. Either way our journey ended with a mile long walk from the train or bus station to Lakefield Road. Here with great relief, and fifteen hours after leaving home, we sat down to breakfast in Auntie Isabel's kitchen.

The weather always seemed to be fine in Llanelli. We spent many days on the beach, my fair skin burning red raw in the strong sun long before we understood the necessity for factor 15 sun cream. I spent many an uncomfortable night sharing a bed with my cousin Heather, my skin aching and blistering with the sun and hurting even more as the pink camomile lotion dried hard on my back. My cousins were all strong swimmers and had more sun-resilient skin than mine. I felt like a wimp alongside them and preferred to go cockle picking or fishing with Uncle Eric rather than flounder around in the water.

A trip to Carmarthen was always on the stocks – usually market day when the pubs were open all day. We took the bus and had dinner with Auntie Vera, the youngest of Dad's sisters, or else we all visited one of the many cafes in the centre of Carmarthen. The cafés were always packed with shoppers and farmers' wives out for the day. The orders were taken by waitresses in black uniforms and white aprons. The meals arrived mysteriously from a far off kitchen on a lift like affair called a dumb waiter. Here we had 'cooked dinner': meat (usually lamb), two vegetables (one of which was mashed but lumpy turnip known in Wales as swede) and mashed potato all covered in gravy followed by a substantial pudding with custard. I did not like the dinner because I did not like the covering of gravy or the excess of custard that covered the pudding. It took me a long time to pluck up the courage to ask for a meal without gravy. All eyes looked at me with incredulity. How could anyone want dinner without gravy? Dinner, it seemed, was defined by gravy.

Dad and Uncle Eric met up with Auntie Vera's window cleaner husband Harry whose ladders were often parked against store windows in Carmarthen whilst he languished in a nearby pub taking refreshment. Once the three got together there was even less window cleaning done, but many pubs were visited.

The aunties and I might track them down in the Spread Eagle, a drinking hole in King Street. Here, I was smuggled in to a back room with the aunties where we had soft drinks and crisps until the men had finished their round in time to catch the bus home. This was a time when women were frowned on for visiting pubs and children were certainly not allowed in.

Dad could handle his drink far better than the uncles could. He was used to much stronger beer in the North East of England. He used to describe Llanelli's Felinfoel Ales as, 'all arms and legs' (no body). As if to prove the point, Dad was always up bright and breezy the following morning, taking a walk to buy a paper while others came too more slowly.

If our trip to Wales on the train was a major event, my impressive brother cycled there and back in 1956. He was 14 when he set off and he had his 15th birthday in Wales on 18 August. He stayed on route in youth hostels and apart from a short time on the train when he hit torrential rain at the end of his journey down, he rode all the way there and back on his own, something you would not let such a young lad do alone today. Down in Llanelli, he and our cousin Winston who had birthdays within three days of one another, cycled around Gower wearing identical black and white checked American cowboy shirts they had for their birthdays.

When I was 13, the parents of a school friend, invited me to go with their family for the October half term week to Blackpool to see the lights. We stayed in a boarding house and spent the days and evenings seeing all the sights of the famous mile. We went up the tower, had tea in the Winter Gardens and went around town at night in a bus when the lights had been switched on.

One day, as a great treat, we went up in a small yellow aeroplane. I bravely hung on to the contents of my boarding house breakfast as we lurched and dived around the tower, out to sea and back again. It only took about ten minutes, but it put me off flying for years.

That night we went to the circus. My knowledge of the circus came from Enid Blyton's 'Circus of Adventure' and my Circus Boy Annual based on the series with Micky Dolenz. The clowns were funny but slightly sinister in their makeup. The trapeze artists thrilled as they swung and leapt across the ring. In those politically incorrect days, the circus still had large captive animals. I loved seeing the slow benign but knowing elephants carefully following one other around each holding the tail of the one in front and sitting to order. The finale, however, was the lions and the lion tamer. In came the lion tamer, cracking his whip and bringing out the lions one by one. Then the last lion came out, but he was grumpy. Every time the lion tamer cracked his whip, the lion snarled and refused his command. After a few abortive attempts at getting the lion to sit on the stool, the lion turned round gave an enormous growl and was horribly sick. I was never more glad to be sitting away from the front, but even towards the back of the big top, you could not evade the appalling smell of a carnivore having disgorged its lunch all over the thankfully sawdust-covered ring. You felt that the lion wanted to say, 'I told you I wasn't well.'

I wanted to go home and have never felt good since about the circus.

Brands, adverts and jingles

World War Two may have stopped in 1945, but its effects still loomed very large for the next 10-15 years in many respects. It is incredible to think that rationing of things we take for granted now did not end until 1954. For example, it was nine years after the war ended when restrictions were lifted on the sale of meat and bacon. Advertising in the way we know it now, only came into its own when there was sufficient choice to woo customers. Back then, supply seemed to be more of an issue than choice. The era of product choice was a long way off in the North East of my childhood.

Sweets, which had started to be rationed in July 1942, were not freely available until 1953 when I was six. From that time on, Dad would call at Waterson's sweetshop in the village and buy me two ounces of some kind of candy after his Sunday lunchtime visit to the Social Club. Dolly mixtures and jelly babies were favourites at first, moving on to chocolate covered raisins or chewing nuts – little hazel-nut sized pieces of chewy toffee coated in very lardy chocolate – as I grew older. The shopkeeper weighed out the sweets from large jars. Chocolate covered or soft sweets were on shelves behind the counter and some hard-boiled ones were placed temptingly in the window. Two ounces were weighed into cone-shaped white paper bags. Four ounces (a quarter) went into square bags and the contents were secured by turning the bags over and twisting the top corners.

There was no such thing as pick and mix and very little that was pre-packed other than chocolate bars and things like Rowntrees fruit gums or pastilles and Spangles. Fry's chocolate cream bars – a white fondant cream coated in dark chocolate and Fry's Five Boys are ones I recall. The latter was a strange bar with each section bearing an outline of a boy's face presenting a different emotion. Murray mints ('...the too-good to hurry mints') were sold individually wrapped and later wrapped as a set in paper tubes.

Some chocolate like Mars Bars were around then, and the chocolate coating seemed thicker than now. 'A Mars a day helps you work, rest and play' was the catchy jingle that gave the consumer the idea that this product was a food as much as a special treat. I occasionally shared slices of a Mars Bar on a Friday night with my godmother as we watched some obscure subtitled film on television.

Products appeared to endure for years at the same price and manufacturers seemed to expect them to judging by the permanence of enamelled advertisements attached to buildings for things like Robin starch (for stiffening collars and cuffs of shirts and cotton sheets). Advertisements were also often painted onto the brickwork of the gable ends of houses and shops. They remained there for years reminding consumers to wash in Sunlight soap or to drink Ringtons' tea.

Marketing boards for basic foods like milk and eggs had catchy slogans like, 'Drinka pinta milka day' and 'Go to work on an egg'. However, compared to nowadays, we were subjected to very little mass advertising. Most of your purchasing decisions were made at the moment you were in the shop and could see the items in front of you. You bought staples like tea, sugar, butter, lard and so on weighed out and packaged in front of you from large containers or blocks of the product rather than as branded pre-packaged amounts. Shop assistants were skilled in making up bags for the tea or sugar, or in cutting just the right amount of greaseproof paper for butter, lard, bacon and so on.

However, slowly, ITV advertisements during and between programmes lodged in your mind and influenced what you bought. In the late 1950s, Unilever launched Sqezy as the first washing up liquid in a soft black polythene container with metal ends. Washing up with this seemed to be a very modern thing to do.

But Sqezy gradually disappeared and the slogan 'Now hands that wash dishes can feel soft as your face with mild green Fairy liquid' persuaded a generation to stop using household soap to wash dishes in favour of a green liquid soap in a plastic bottle that persists to this day.

'You'll wonder where the yellow went when you brush your teeth with Pepsodent' was catchy enough to stick in my mind even though it did not change our buying habits from Macleans ('Have you Macleaned your teeth today?').

Snack foods were largely confined to salted peanuts and the potato crisp. Smiths Crisps were sold in bags with the salt separate in the packet in a twist of dark blue waxed paper. Sometimes the production went wrong and you could get several twists of salt or none at all in some packs. I once tried to make some crisps at home in the oven carefully slicing the potato with a potato peeler and putting the slices coated in fat on a tray in the oven. They were not a success.

Gradually, magazines targeted women and girls with sensuous advertisement for essential cleaning products. Soap became desirable beauty items such as pink Camay and the enduring Cussons Imperial leather. Around Christmas time, you could buy sets of Imperial Leather products like shaving soap in bowls and bath cubes. The soap seemed to last a long time and you could make the last little piece go further by sticking it on to the reverse side of the new bar when both pieces were wet.

Tea was the main drink at home – Ringtons', of course, with milk and sugar until I was 12. At this point, I gave up sugar in drinks for Lent and never took it again. The other drinks I had regularly were Milo and Ribena. Milo was a chocolate malt drink developed in the 1930s as a way of getting vitamins, minerals and milk into growing children. Ribena was made from the juice of blackcurrants and was a good source of vitamin C. I realised years later that it gets its name from Ribes the Latin name for currants. I used to make a cup of hot Ribena last for ages when given it as a suppertime drink, much to my brother's annoyance as he had to see that I went to bed at a reasonable hour. The 1950s rather un-PC TV advert showed a couple of dancing blackcurrants dressed as black and white minstrels.

Instant coffee appeared in our home around the early 1960s probably about the time when my brother was at university developing cosmopolitan tastes. We had Nescafé in a very small tin containing about an ounce of the precious brown powder. In truth, although I liked the coffee served in Italian coffee bars, I did not really like instant coffee as made at home, but it became the cool thing to drink when with your teenage friends.

Fashion

During the week, until I was about 13, I would simply continue to wear my school uniform in the evenings. It never entered my head that I should have other clothes for wearing during the week, especially as I knew how much the full outfit for Henry Smith's had cost. At weekends, I wore trousers, a jumper or T-shirt and a zipped up jacket or duffel coat, depending on the time of the year. I hated having invitations to parties as I had nothing fashionable to wear and felt very self-conscious in the few rather dated and unflattering clothes that I had. My godmother was very good in taking me to Stockton or Middlesbrough to buy the main things that I needed such as underwear that was not the school issue navy blue knickers and vests. She would say to my Dad that I needed 'various things' and to his great relief would offer to take me shopping. He could not get his wallet out fast enough as long as he did not have to go with me, as he would not have known where to start.

Shopping for clothes was done mainly in Stockton, where there was some choice – only the Co-op in Billingham sold clothes to any extent. We would visit Marks and Spencer's or a family owned departmental store called Robinson's. More rarely, we might go to Middlesbrough and visit Binns, another large department store, or go to C&A, a large Dutch department store that sold all kinds of clothing. I remember getting a new coat from C&A because a boy from school had asked me to go to the cinema with him. Why I had to have a new coat to go to the cinema is not clear, but my godmother was determined that I should look smart on this landmark occasion. The coat was a sort of brown and black mixture with double-breasted buttons in mock bronze and slanted side pockets with flaps. I also had new brown shoes with chisel toes and a very small heel, quite unlike the sensible flat lace ups I had to wear for school. With the shoes, and in the days before tights, came a pair of nylons and a suspender belt. I was the business.

My interest in clothes blossomed further when I realised that I could buy patterns and material and make my own clothes in the latest styles for a fraction of what it would cost to buy them. From about the age of 15 until well into my thirties, I made a lot of what I wore: from blouses, skirts and dresses to ambitious suits and even a full length lined maxi coat.

From 1963, a trip to Stockton on a Saturday would not be complete without visiting Robinson's departmental store to look at paper patterns and the market to look at lengths of material. The main brands of patterns made by Simplicity, Butterick, McCalls and Style ranged in price from about 3/6d for a simple skirt or blouse to 5/- for something more complex like a suit or a set of skirts or blouses. Every so often, I would buy a Vogue pattern. Those patterns were for more complex and designer-based fashion and the price of them was often double that of more simple designs. Some of the patterns were sponsored by named designers like Mary Quant or Jean Muir, these too were more expensive but highly desirable. Many a Saturday night was spent with the furniture pushed back as I crawled about the living room floor pinning the pattern to the material and cutting out the shapes to make up the following afternoon.

Work and money

If work is defined as receiving some sort of payment in exchange for your time and effort, then my first experience of work was 'getting the money back' on empty lemonade bottles that I took to The Dairy, a shop on the corner of Teesdale Avenue. The shop had long since ceased to be a dairy and was more a tiny general store that sold groceries and greengrocery. The shopkeeper, Mr Allen, gave 3d for the lemonade bottles and 1d or 2d for the bleach bottles. I much favoured the lemonade bottles not just because we were paid more for them but because I was afraid of getting drops of bleach on my clothes. This was recycling at its best. The bottles were not crushed, melted and reformed but washed out, sterilised, refilled and relabelled before being resold. The money we earned was usually recycled in Mr Allen's shop so he was an all-round winner.

One day, I learned about saving. You could buy saving stamps at school that bore pictures of Prince Charles or Princess Anne. As I recall, the more expensive ones had a picture of the Prince and the cheaper ones, his sister. The stamps were stuck in a book and could be redeemed later when the money was needed for a special occasion. This was fine and probably taught me about being able to afford something through thrift, but then I learned about the Post Office savings account. It was a revelation that people would give you money for leaving some of your money with them. I could not really understand this as I imagined that my money was simply building up in a separate drawer with my name on it somewhere in the bowels of the Post Office. I had not understood about investing. I opened my Post Office account with five shillings (about 25p today). You could put in very small amounts and I enjoyed seeing the contents grow supplemented by the interest that was added periodically.

I realised later as a teenager that I received quite a lot of pocket money compared with other school friends. Dad gave me money for helping in the home with housework, shopping, washing and ironing. If I did a big job, like wallpapering, I was paid extra for that.

With that as a backcloth, I had a summer job cleaning for a woman who lived in one of the houses on the by-pass in the old village. Things started well enough but quickly deteriorated when the woman followed me from room to room pointing our bits that she thought that I had missed. Considering I had been cleaning at home since I was nine years of age, I felt she might have more confidence in me. This was my first experience of feeling exploited and I decided that the ten shillings reward was not enough to compensate for the working conditions – a good early lesson.

When I was a young teenager, Dad and his mate Paddy set up a window cleaning business. They went out in the evenings and at weekends to do the window cleaning. Their initial investment was to buy a handcart to transport the ladders and some chamois leather cloths and dusters. They also had some leaflets printed in the village advertising the Acme Window Cleaning Company. I was given the job (and roped in friends to help) of taking the leaflets round the doors and collecting in the replies from anyone who wanted a window cleaner. The response around the ICI estate was miserable. The business kept going mainly by cleaning the windows of the shops along Station Road, the bigger houses on The Green and a few houses in the streets adjacent to the old village. For years Dad saved up the extra money earned to help fund my brother, and later, me, through university.

One summer holiday I was enlisted to help with the window cleaning, as shown by the photograph right.

All went well until the friend who was helping me let the triangular ladder slip whereupon it bent the leaded lights of a customer's

Window cleaning Roy's furniture store Billingham Green.

window in Sunnybrow Avenue. That was the end of that as a holiday job.

Later that same summer, I tried my hand at selling ice cream. A friend and I rented a small Ford Anglia specially designed by Walls for selling their ice cream. He could drive and I could not, so my job was to sit inside the all-too-small cabin and sell the goods. The van had a tiny insulated container which acted as a fridge once you had put in it a block of dry ice (solid carbon dioxide). The morning routine was to drive to ICI and buy a block of dry ice at a cost of ten shillings. Armed with the activated fridge, we then went to the wholesaler and bought our day's supply of ice cream. The profit on ice cream was made by selling high volumes. With this in mind, we stocked up mainly on ice-lollies and small paper-wrapped rectangular blocks of ice cream. We sold these with two wafers or a rectangular-shaped cone. You made an old penny on each ice cream that you sold. The most expensive stock item retailed at a shilling but could be bought wholesale at seven old pennies. This was the strawberry flavoured ice-lolly with ice cream inside. Feeling very optimistic about the day, we also took a few of these on board.

Off we set looking for a suitable place to pitch and sell. What could be difficult about selling ice cream to children in the middle of the summer holiday? The answer is many things. First, we struggled to find anywhere to stop and sell without being told to push off by men who sold ice cream for a living and not just as a summer hobby. Mafiosi who had been working that particular patch since the war told us to move, or else. Eventually, ever aware of our dwindling block of dry ice, we settled on the Blue Hall estate in Norton. Oddly, nobody else seemed to be there. We soon attracted a curious crowd of children but they regarded Walls ice creams as too posh to afford and all they wanted was broken wafers for nothing. To add to all this, it rained heavily, weather likely to keep even the keenest ice cream eaters in doors. That night, we went home with most of our stock. With no alternative (we had not envisaged having any ice cream let by the end of the day) we had to put our stock in the icebox of our fridge. Sadly, the elderly Bosch proved to be too warm to keep the ice cream in its fully solid state. Despite a quick trip to ICI the following morning, even the dry ice could not save us, or the ice cream, which simply set in a rather unattractive uneven state. That day, as if things could not get worse, the van broke down and we were pushed down the road by a crowd of jeering children bought off with handfuls of wafers. The cost of the van, the dry ice, and the failure to keep our assets frozen, led us to abandon the project and we never sold our expensive lollies.

One summer holiday, Dad came home and said that the manager of Billingham Motors wanted someone to work in the petrol station. The job entailed taking the money for the petrol sold, but in the days before self-service pumps, you also had to put the fuel into the cars' tanks. You went out as soon as a car or lorry drew up and asked how many gallons of which type of fuel was needed. Diesel, or derv as it was known, was served from a pump well away from the petrol. This measure served to keep what was then a very smelly product as far away as possible and prevented people from putting in the wrong fuel to petrol engines.

No one liked serving the derv customers, partly because they were often lorry drivers who made lewd and sexist remarks and partly because the fuel smelled so badly. If you got so much as a drop of the stuff on you or your clothes it took ages to get rid of the smell of rotten fish. I remember going into a shop in the village after finishing work and people turning and staring at me when I had been serving on the derv pump that day.

As you can see in the picture below of me mimicking the Regent advertisement, different pumps were used for different grades of petrol.

Break time at Billingham Motors. Houses in Station Road and Conifer Crescent in the background.

In these days of fuel costing more than £1 per litre, the prices in the 60s bring tears to your eyes. Even the most expensive was less than 30p a gallon (5 litres).

Filling up the tank with petrol was not always easy and you soon learned that some cars were slow fillers (Morris Minors and the Standard 8). These cars developed an air lock very quickly and the petrol spat back if you tried to put it in the tank at anything other than a slow drizzle. Petrol on the floor still had to be paid for by the customer, so if this happened you were likely to have a complaint.

After you had filled up the tank with petrol, some drivers would expect you to check the oil and fill that up if needed as well as doing the same for the water level in the radiator. In the days before all cars had windscreen washers, some drivers would expect cleaning the windscreen with a sponge as a further free service.

Another incentive to buy your fuel at Billingham Motors was the issue of Green Shield Stamps that came with your purchase. These were the forerunner of things like store loyalty cards or Air Miles. You collected a green stamp for every six pence you spent and stuck it in books with an orange cover. When you had enough books, you could exchange them for gifts from a catalogue. Most people exchanged them for things like mugs or glasses but you could save for attractive electrical items like TVs and kitchen equipment. You would have had to spend a great deal to get enough stamps for a gift of any worth. In fact, in an idle moment we once worked it out that you could have probably bought a house in Billingham for the money you would have had to spend to get a TV from saving enough Green Shield stamps.

In 1967 during the summer vacation, I was offered a short-term job with the National Coal Board (NCB). The job came about as a consequence of the Aberfan Disaster the previous October. The coal mining industry in County Durham was ending in the late 60s and many of the pit heaps in the area had already greened over. My job was to go out each day and carry out surveys of what was growing on different aspects of these Durham spoil heaps and to draw conclusions as to what the NCB might plant to make the pit heaps in South Wales more stable. This job was well paid. I earned £12 a week. To put it in perspective, each of my weekly earnings paid for 6 weeks rent on my share of a student rented terraced house in West Jesmond, Newcastle.

This was my first taste of independent work as I could organise my own time provided I came up with the findings by a set date. I had to work out the public transport routes to places like Shotton and Tudhoe, keep a list of expenses incurred and write up my findings each evening. Once at each pit village I took compass readings around the pit heaps to work out which way the heaps were facing. To the amusement of former miners walking their dogs, I carried out surveys on all of the plants, assessing how well each grew on every side of the heap. At the end of a visit, I used a card to record information about each pit heap. The cards had holes punched around the edges. The holes variously represented an aspect of the pit heap, a species of plant that I had found there and the frequency and cover the species afforded. This sort of analysis would be done nowadays with a simple computer programme but I did all this manually armed with a ball point pen, a pair of scissors and some knitting needles to sort out which cards showed similarities.

By the time I moved down to South Wales in the mid-80s, the pit heaps were greening over, but whether or not the work I did had any influence, I never knew.

A few final words

One Friday in late September 1965, I left Henry Smith's School and Hartlepool for the last time. That same weekend I left home in Billingham to go to university and only returned during holiday periods. I was 17 years old. I had intended to go much further afield, but, in the event, I joined my brother in Newcastle.

The Billingham I left was probably at a peak in the years between the late 50s and early 60s. Billingham was synonymous with ICI, home to the largest chemical industry in the Commonwealth. Employment rates in the area were high and the money and pensions offered by ICI were felt to be second to none. ICI had built its new multi-storey main offices just along the road from home, at the end of Central Avenue. The building's unusual paternoster lifts were the talk of the town. ICI's sports' stadium close by was the only place in the North East able to host international athletics events. The College of Further Education was the first of its kind in western Europe. The campus school project of the 1960s with its co-located grammar school, secondary modern schools and junior schools was an important development that tried to put into practice key aspects of the 1944 Education Act.

In that period, Billingham Urban District Council distributed a booklet to all homes in the area describing the council's plans for further transformation. 'The Miracle of Billingham' told in words and pictures what the residents could expect in the 1960s that would add to the town's many achievements.

The focus of Billingham was shifting rapidly away from the village and its surrounding ICI housing estates, to the town centre, north of the railway line and west of the A19. Sadly, no one had the vision to keep the village in tune with its ancient church and a village green setting.

Some of the places around The Green, which nowadays might have been modernised in a style more in keeping with the time in which

Billingham Green pre-1970 when the school (left) was still there. The row of cottages (to the top of the picture) were later replaced by flat-roofed maisonettes.

they were built, were simply razed to the ground. In their place came flat-roofed maisonettes.

Concrete was the material of choice in the town centre and its new shopping units, multi-story housing, pedestrianised areas, and free, purpose-built two-storey car parks. When Her Majesty the Queen opened the Forum in 1967 leisure centres were not commonplace in towns around the UK, and the Forum was no ordinary leisure centre. With its ice rink, an Olympic-sized swimming pool and a theatre that attracted stars and those keen to make their name, it was a new concept in sport and the arts.

The International Folklore Festival took hold in the 60s and it was exciting and novel each year during August to see street performers from all over

'The Family' by Edward Bainbridge Copnall.

the world in the Town Square.

Arriving home with former school friends during vacations from university and college, we were amazed at the speed and the extent of the changes taking place in Billingham. Nightclubs appeared which drew famous acts, showbiz people stayed at the Billingham Arms and we heard tales of their exploits. The names of new public houses (The Telstar and The Astronaut) reflected the times. Parents of friends became members of the first municipal golf club in the country. Billingham also boasted an art gallery and an iconic street sculpture called 'The Family' by Edward Bainbridge Copnall.

By Christmas 1967, a new Billingham seemed to have arrived. The town had developed multi-storey living, a two-storey pedestrianised shopping centre with access for the disabled and parents with pushchairs and prams. There were leisure and arts facilities to rival far larger places around the UK.

The Astronaut pub at the west end of the Town Centre, Billingham with the two storey car park to the right. ICI towers and chimneys can just be seen on the right in the far distance.

Although I have not lived in the North East for more than 40 years, I have always felt a connection with it through my family and my godmother who 'adopted' me as part of her family. My father lived there until the mid-80s and my brother lived there until his too early death in 2010. This book is dedicated with love to all of them.